PRACTICAL
NLP FOR MANAGERS

PRACTICAL NLP FOR MANAGERS

❖

Ian McDermott and Joseph O'Connor

Gower

Published by
Gower Publishing Limited
Gower House
Croft Road
Aldershot
Hampshire GU11 3HR
England

Gower
Old Post Road
Brookfield
Vermont 05036
USA

Reprinted 1997, 1998

Ian McDermott and Joseph O'Connor have asserted their right under the Copyright, Designs and Patents Act 1988 to be identified as the authors of this work.

British Library Cataloguing in Publication Data

McDermott, Ian
    Practical NLP for managers
    1. Neurolinguistic programming 2. Management 3. Success in business
    I. Title II. O'Connor, Joseph, 1948
    658.4´09

    ISBN 0-566-07671-3

Library of Congress Cataloging-in-Publication Data

McDermott, Ian.
    Practical NLP for managers / Ian McDermott and Joseph O'Connor.
        p.   cm.
    Includes index.
    1. Communication in personnel management. 2. Neurolinguistic programming. 3. Interpersonal relations. 4. Nonverbal communication. I. O'Connor, Joseph. II. Title.
    HF5549.5C6M324 1998
    658.3—dc20   95-49393
                                                                      CIP

Typeset in Garamond by Photoprint, Torquay, Devon and printed in Great Britain by Biddles Ltd, Guildford.

CONTENTS

PREFACE

'Microsoft's only factory asset is human imagination.'
Fred Moody, *The New York Times Magazine* 25 August 1991

People are the greatest resource of any organization. What does this mean in practice? All ideas, plans and products begin in the human imagination. Can you manage the human imagination? If so, how? Or do we have to look beyond management? This book explores these questions in a practical way.

BEYOND MANAGING – WHAT?

More managing only harder? No. Managing is a means to an end, an end with measurable achievements and results. People produce results – you and others working together, towards goals that you believe are worthwhile. These goals can be lost in day-to-day problems. When you are knee deep in crocodiles it is hard to remember that you went in to drain the swamp. A hard day battling crocodiles is certainly tiring, may be necessary, yet leaves you curiously unfulfilled. 'Beyond managing' rather than 'Beyond management' emphasizes that managing is something you *do* every day. Managing is a huge subject and this book touches on many aspects.

Managing is often focused on problems – what goes wrong and how to put it right – so there is a constant stream of new problem-solving management ideas. New management practices are introduced; sometimes they work, sometimes they do not. Sometimes it seems that changes are simply being made for the sake of it. Many management initiatives are greeted with scepticism, and rightly so, when the instigators of the initiative expect everyone in the company except themselves to accept the new practice. Quality standards may result in a superbly documented, but otherwise unchanged, flow of problems.

This book does not present another different management initiative, but looks at central principles. What is common to all systems of management? People. Seventy per cent of management tasks involve dealing with people. These people are your bosses, your peers, your team, your customers and – dare we say it – yourself. A manager is not a shell of tasks and functions, but a real person with hopes and feelings. Unless management practices take those human qualities into consideration they will fail in the short term rather than the long term. A good idea is only as good as its implementation; people make it real in practice. The main task of managing day by day is to motivate and deal with people to achieve goals.

Any system of management that does not take the feelings and hopes of people into account will not work. This is often taken for granted rather than put into practice. What is needed is a method for bringing together the goals and structures of business management with human skills to deal with the diverse people who actually do the work. This book aims to supply it. Structure without people is soulless, attending to the people without structure tends to slide slowly or quickly into warm, fuzzy chaos.

This is a practical book, but not a prescriptive one. You are the expert at your job. Our aim is to suggest choices for you to achieve what you want, in a time of rapid business change. The pressures of developments in the 1990s continue to transform the structure of organizations to meet the fast, mutating global market. One result is that organizations have become flatter, and quicker to respond to the needs of the customer. Information technology has speeded up what was possible and opened new possibilities. A necessary empowerment is taking place where people at every level of the company are given decision-making powers, responsibility and accountability. The learning organization is the new model for business, and for companies to learn, the people within them must learn too.

All this could simply add another layer of complexity to the manager's already intricate task. What do these changes mean in everyday practice? We look at three levels:

O   First, the organizational level. New business structures need new ways of thinking, or mental models. However, replacing one way of thinking with another will only take you as far as the next change in business structure. This is a short-term view. What is needed, and what we aim to provide in this book, is a way of thinking that is a step higher than any particular organizational structure: a way of thinking that is flexible enough to deal with any management system, just as a mathematical rule of addition can solve all the possible different adding problems.

O   Secondly, dealing with people. This is where management theory meets practice (and sometimes comes off second best). Decisions, motivation, appraisal, clear communication and coaching are all part of managing. Any practical book on management must deal with these so-called 'soft' issues (however, they lead to very hard problems if neglected).

O   Thirdly, you – the manager. How do you express yourself through your work? People who cannot manage themselves will not be able to manage others. Part of managing involves providing a model and a motivation for your people by being yourself. Leadership begins with leading yourself. So this book brings you into the picture. Just as we know from physics that observers are part of the world they observe, so the manager is part of the organization, and the days are over when management is treated in isolation as if it was something you do to others.

How does Neuro-Linguistic Programming or NLP fit into the managing process? NLP is the study of the structure of subjective experience. It is how we make up our world – our unique experience of who we are, what we do and how we experience others. How do we think? How do we learn? How do we become stressed? How do we communicate? Any activity that involves relating to others involves NLP. As befits its title, NLP concerns language: how language affects our thoughts and actions. We use language to communicate, influence and motivate, so NLP is about how to influence. NLP answers the questions it raises in a unique way – by modelling successful performers. Already it has studied many outstanding communicators, managers, salespeople and educators to find the patterns they have in common. This means you can learn and use the patterns in your own life to achieve the results that are important to you.

We do not intend to tell you about NLP in the abstract. This would be the equivalent of a salesperson boring you with innumerable features. You want benefits, so all the NLP here will be in the context of management applications.

HOW TO USE THIS BOOK

What you bring to this book determines its worth as much as what we have put into it. There are eleven chapters. The first sets the scene, bringing together a wide view of business trends that we believe will accelerate throughout the 1990s. It examines how organizations are changing both in structure and function, under the pressure of technology and expanding, diversified and competitive global markets.

Chapters 2 and 3 look at different perspectives as analytical tools for understanding the organization as a system, and building rapport and trust at work. Thinking about management as managing systems and relationships sheds new light on many management problems.

Chapters 4 and 5 are concerned with goals or outcomes, both individual and organizational, and how to translate the company mission into achievable goal-focused projects. What does the company mission statement mean operationally, to the people who work closest to the customers?

Chapters 6 and 7 discuss values. We believe that organizational values are an extremely important and neglected part of management. All organizations have values, but not everyone is aware of what they are. These chapters also clarify individual values; they are our strongest motivation, we work for what is important to us. Chapter 8 deals in more detail with motivation and leadership. The final three chapters concentrate on the individual, how we think, what we pay attention to, and how we create our internal state. Knowing this gives you more influence with others and yourself.

You can move around the book and read what interests you in any order. However, reading Chapters 1 and 2 first will give you a guide and reference for getting the most out of the others. We have spoken to many managers about what they would want in a practical book on management, and this is the result. We hope it is useful. Both of us work as trainers and consultants with companies, and we draw on this experience for most of the examples. Sometimes we write together about these experiences, although perhaps only one of us was involved. We have also drawn on the experience of friends and colleagues with their permission. We have changed names where appropriate and withheld names where necessary.

The English language has yet to find an acceptable pronoun that combines both 'he' and 'she', so we will use and interchange both freely to avoid some awkward and ungrammatical constructions.

Ian McDermott and Joseph O'Connor

ACKNOWLEDGEMENTS

We would like to thank the many people who helped us with this book.

We acknowledge our debt to Richard Bandler and John Grinder, co-founders of NLP. Also Robert Dilts, one of the leading developers and originator of the Logical Levels model.

Thank you to our editor at Gower, Malcolm Stern, and to Allie Clarke for her cartoons that so enhance the presentation.

Many friends and colleagues provided material and help. Thank you to Bob Janes and Duane Lakin, and especially to Manoj Chawla and the development team for sharing their work on the Fire project.

Finally, thanks to our many colleagues and students for their examples, especially Michael Trigg, Ian Tibbles, Vivian Phelps-Tate, Tony O'Connell, Karyl Shone, Thelma Aye, Anna McQuaid, David Upsher, Gill Norman-Bruce, John Donnelly and Patricia Boissons. What we have fashioned from the help and contributions we have received remains our responsibility.

Ian McDermott and Joseph O'Connor

1
SETTING THE SCENE

❖

'There is nothing more difficult to take in hand, more perilous to
conduct, or more uncertain in its success, than to take the lead in the
introduction of a new order of things, because the innovator has for
enemies all those who have done well under the old conditions, and
lukewarm defenders in those who may do well under the new.'

Machiavelli, 1469–1527, *The Prince*[1]

The 1990s have been, and continue to be, a stormy time to be in
business. Opportunities and dangers are balanced in a global game
of snakes and ladders with millions of players, challenging managers
in new ways. Change and development at an ever increasing rate seem the
only constants. Management is using advances in communication technology, computers and software to do what it had done before, only faster,
while the nature of the game has been changing. Hot-wiring the dinosaur
with new information and communication technology was at best an
interim solution, now it is a recipe for disaster.

Organizations now face rapidly changing, decentralized, global markets
that seem to shift on the whim of fashion. Some goals remain the same:
commitment to the customer, the ability to extract the best from your people
and yourself, and the success of your organization in the market place
whether it offers cars, financial advice, software or soft drinks. These goals
are stable, but the ways to achieve them are changing and require flexibility
of thinking. Has our thinking kept pace with our technological advance? Not
yet. We still use an organizational model that was the height of fashion in
the mid-seventeenth century: a pyramid. The decision maker at the top, and

distinct production areas with their own head, followed by a hierarchy of managers whose jobs are defined by function. Time to move on.

THE ABILITY TO PREDICT YESTERDAY

In a world where a book can be published on the Gulf War a week after the ceasefire[2] (from manuscript to finished book often takes up to a year), competitive advantage comes from being first to market. Not once, but consistently over a range of products. Your competitors are never far behind. Speed wins, and it is tiring too. The pyramid organizations are simply too slow to react. By the time the planning, costing and information has worked its way onto the desk of someone empowered to make a decision, and the decision worked its way down again, probably becoming enmeshed in office politics as it goes, the opportunity has either disappeared or been snapped up by a nimbler competitor. Managers like to gather as much information as possible before committing themselves and their organization to any course of action. The cost of mistakes can be high,

but so too can the cost of not acting. No decision, no mistakes, but perhaps no sale either.

With the market moving so fast, the ability to gather feedback is essential. You cannot respond if you do not have information. The best feedback is immediate. Research that gives you the ability to predict yesterday is not very valuable. You need to know what is happening today, in order to make the intelligent guesses about tomorrow that have to be initiated now. The more distant the feedback the less use it becomes and the more difficult it is to connect to your action.

Organizations are looking for managers prepared to take risks, and are rewarding them for doing so. Such empowerment has its downside. When bureaucratic hierarchy has been the guiding principle and people have been used to external limits, removing these limits can result in people drowning as well as swimming. Power needs to be dispersed so that self-discipline can replace imposed discipline, and bureaucracy is replaced with shared vision and shared values, otherwise empowerment is a recipe for chaos.

FLATTEN OR BE FLATTENED

Companies are flattening their structure to better deal with the changing markets. They spread outwards into networks of separate parts, and these are often geographically spread. The horizontal corporation is increasingly with us. In a flatter organization there are fewer levels of decision making. This has two consequences. Firstly, people are empowered to make decisions that before they would have had to refer to a 'higher' authority. Teams are the foundation of the horizontal corporation, organized round processes not departments. Secondly, middle management is squeezed and now is likely to be taking on new responsibilities. They will be more involved at the customer interface, and will also have to take decisions that previously were referred up the chain of command. Some traditional managers' functions are disappearing, while others are being taken on. The hierarchy is flattened partly by combining tasks that were previously unrelated. The manager's position has become more ambiguous, less easy to pin down. In a hierarchy lines of authority are clear. Now managers need to rely on influencing skills in their work. Security no longer comes from being employed, but from being employable.

TEAMS AND NETWORKS

Goal-focused project teams are being used increasingly in management to solve problems, bring a product to market, and work with clients, suppliers and customers. Teams can be created quickly, and when they work well, they do tasks in a fraction of the time it took previously, when much more of the organization was involved. These teams cut across departments and across functions. There is a whole new set of managerial skills needed to manage, participate in and lead these teams to get the best from them. Capability and expertise are more highly valued; one of the paradoxes of so much information becoming available is that now even experts cannot keep track of it all. It is much more important to be able to find the information you need for a particular project, and to learn skills on the job itself. When required, expert knowledge can be contracted out, and formal and informal networks become increasingly important.

The skills of a successful project manager should not be underestimated. Managers need negotiating, influencing and listening skills to gain the commitment and action of key team members. They need to be able to deal with details, as well as be able to relate them to the wider picture. They need networking skills. They need to learn quickly.

In 1988 a four-year study of over 400 managers was published.[3] It suggested that a manager's activity fell into four primary categories. Firstly, routine communications and paperwork. Secondly, traditional activities such as planning, decision making and controlling. Thirdly, human resource management: motivating, disciplining, staff training and development. Finally, networking: establishing and maintaining contacts. Even in 1988 those managers defined as successful, that is who achieved results, spent about 48 per cent of their time networking, as opposed to the 12 per cent spent by the less successful managers. In the 1990s, networking has become even more important. Teams are assembled from people who are geographically and functionally separate, as the organization spreads out.

TECHNOLOGY NETWORKS MANAGEMENT

Computer technology is a good metaphor for the way management has changed since the 1970s. First there was the massive monolithic mainframe computer, the symbol of dependence. The information was stored centrally. After a while this gave way to the personal desktop computer, many of which are more powerful than the huge mainframes they replaced. Workers became independent. Management became more entrepreneurial and individualistic. Now we have a client server model and the Internet as a potent symbol of the interdependence of management, which brings its own special problems, opportunities and responsibilities.

Networking is how information flows, and information, that great intangible, is made from our imagination. When you buy a computer you pay most of your money for the human imagination that built and conceived it. Information must be freely available throughout the company, and quickly. That is a fundamental part of empowerment, along with the creation of viable project-based teams. The 'need to know' principle now works the opposite way. Assume everyone has a need to know. They probably do. Part of empowerment is unclogging the corporate arteries so that information can flow freely. Empowerment will fail if people are given responsibility without the information on which to base decisions.

HIGH TECH AND HIGH TOUCH

Managers need to influence people at many different levels in a flatter organization. They will find themselves working with consultants, customers, independent experts and suppliers. Communication skills will become even more important. Paradoxically, the more 'high tech' we become, the more 'high touch' becomes important. When British Airways and British Caledonian merged, the chairman, Lord King, and the managing director, Sir Colin Marshall, were concerned that the line employees were unhappy about the resulting arrangements. The answer, according to the research they commissioned, was very simple. The line workers felt the work they had put in to make the merger a success was unappreciated. The solution was a huge party for all 40,000 staff running every night for a fortnight. 'Thank you' is so simple to say and do. It is also simple to overlook in a management culture that often assumes adequate pay and conditions are sufficient to keep people happy and appreciated in their work. Adequate pay and conditions are important, and only a starting point. Even when pay and conditions are excellent, appreciation and recognition make a difference. You will remember times when your own experiences of being recognized and appreciated for your achievements made a difference to you. You may also know what it feels like to be overlooked.

THE LEARNING ORGANIZATION

The term 'learning organization' is much in vogue. Learning links individual change to organizational change. We all have an inner drive to learn, to own and take pride in our work. We all want to achieve our goals and be recognized for our achievements. A learning organization is one that creates the conditions where its people can learn; it is one in which people at all levels individually and collectively increase their capacity to produce results they really care about.

An influential exposition of the learning organization is *The Fifth Discipline – The Art and Practice of the Learning Organisation* by Peter Senge, director of the systems thinking and organizational learning programme at the Sloan School of Management, Massachusetts Institute of Technology (MIT). Senge outlines five key disciplines that are needed to create a learning organization.

The first is building shared vision: the process of creating an organizational purpose and identity that inspires and motivates all the members of the organization. The second is team learning: the conditions for teams to be effective. The third is mental models: the unconscious beliefs of individuals and groups that shape their behaviour and decisions. Management decisions are driven as much (sometimes more) by emotions and beliefs as logic and rationality. The discipline here is learning how to surface limiting beliefs and change them into more empowering ones, leading to better decisions and action. Senge calls the fourth discipline personal mastery. This concerns expertise, not dominance: mastery in the sense of the master craftsman or woman who has a lifelong commitment to improving their skills, motivation and satisfaction which comes from within.

The fifth discipline of the title is systemic thinking, very different from our traditional linear thought process. Thinking systemically about an organization looks at the connection of its parts, and sees a process of development rather than separated snapshots. It sees loops where linear thinking sees only straight lines. It looks at long-term consequences. Decisions have future results that are often overlooked, because decision and result are widely separated in time and place. This is as true in companies as it is in medicine and weather forecasting. Systemic thinking can show how a company structure can create problems and how the consequences of managers' decisions show up elsewhere in the system, sometimes coming back to create the very problem they were designed to alleviate.

In a sense the term 'learning organization' is misleading. It is not an all-or-nothing state. You do not suddenly become a learning organization. Organizations, like people, do learn all the time; they change and adapt due to the decisions of individuals within them in response to the pressures from without. The questions to ask are:

○   What do they learn?
○   How can we increase organizational learning in a way that increases the wellbeing of the people within the organization and the effectiveness of the organization in the market place?

○ What are we doing that is promoting useful learning?
○ What are we currently doing that is stopping learning from taking place?

The skills you can develop by reading this book – understanding and working with people and teams, looking at the business on a deeper level than fighting crocodiles in the swamp, and extending your influence – are precisely those needed to foster a learning organization, and to thrive within one.

All of Senge's disciplines involve learning thinking skills, acting effectively and continuously improving what we do. This is a manager's territory. The quality of the people and their ability to learn is the most important part of competitive success. People do the best they can, given the system they are in. The question becomes how can you create an environment where people can give their best and learn?

SEMCO

Semco is an engineering firm based in Sao Paulo, Brazil. It manufactures a wide range of products: huge industrial pumps, dishwashers and air-conditioning cooling units. Semco is an extreme example of organizational change. When Ricardo Semler took over as CEO from his father in 1980, Semco was a traditional company full of written procedures and with a pyramidal structure. Ten years later it was transformed. Factory workers now set their own production quotas and take responsibility for meeting them. They help design the product and the marketing plans. Semco managers have unusual freedom in the business strategy they pursue. They set their own salaries, and everybody knows what they are; all financial information is openly discussed and any Semco worker has access to the accounting books. Semler says explicitly he wants everyone at Semco to be self-sufficient and able to make decisions. 'Success,' he says, 'means not having to make them myself.'

Brazil has experienced very high inflation and a disorganized economic policy, yet productivity at Semco has increased sevenfold. Profits have increased by 500 per cent. They have a backlog of over 2,000 job applications. The firm has attracted international interest. Executives from IBM, General Motors, Ford, Kodak and many others have visited the plant to see for themselves how Semco works.

Semco has applied many of the ideas that are changing companies in the direction of learning organizations:

○ Employ the best people. People who are good learners, respond well to others, network and obtain results. This is true at every level of the organization.

- ○ Shared values make many rules unnecessary.
- ○ Rules and procedures are kept to a minimum. (Semler says feed the rule book to the shredder; although in practice he adopted a less radical approach, simply withdrawing the rule books, and saying they were being revised and reissued. They never were.)
- ○ Trust people. The fewer rules and procedures, the more people have to be trusted anyway.
- ○ Empower people to make decisions and to be accountable for them.
- ○ Goal-focused teams are the normal way of working. These teams are responsible for a whole project. In Semco there are no assembly line teams. When the team has a total project to oversee and carry to completion, they can see a real result at the end of it. This encourages responsibility and ownership of the project. It fosters pride in achievement.
- ○ Information is in the open.

RESISTANCE TO CHANGE

Managing in a time of organizational change is not easy, and never has been. Constant development means continuous learning in the organization: to adopt better structures, better processes, and respond more quickly to changes in the market place. This constant development, however, clashes with repeatable management procedures. Any system needs structures that keep it stable, or it will collapse at the first challenge. These structures and procedures are important and cannot be disregarded. They work against change, any change. Resistance to change always contains something valuable. Without a structure, some stability and repeatable procedures, an organization cannot become good at anything. There has to be a balance of stability and development. Even when the company structure stays stable, the people in it can continue to learn.

Part of the structure that keeps the organization stable is the people within it and the way they react. Companies recruit people who fit in with the established culture and ethos, and the established way of doing things. There is a feel good factor in working and implementing the old set of organizational values, which means that decisions based on learning and change are likely initially to feel wrong to managers. The decision-making strategy will be channelled in the old ways. So if a decision feels wrong, it could be right (but not necessarily). If a decision feels right, it could well be wrong (but not necessarily). Who said this was easy?

What can you do? It seems hopeless. The more you try to change and adapt, the more the system pushes back, and it is likely to feel wrong to boot. The answer is to change levels. To achieve change at the organizational level, learning must take place on an individual level. Perhaps your greatest task as a manager is to allow this to happen for yourself and others that you have influence with and responsibility for.

LOSING CONTROL

The word 'control' has an interesting history. In the Middle Ages, servants helped themselves from their masters' coffers, and their accounts were checked against a duplicate roll. The master could verify payments against this *contra rotulus* – the second roll. Woe betide the servant if his record did not match the 'second roll' – the control. There is no organizational second roll. Effective managers concentrate on what they can influence – people, including of course, themselves.

To achieve organizational results, you first have to realize you have no direct control over the organization. Control comes from information. Complete control comes from complete information, which you will never have. The promise of more and more specialist magazines, surveys, sophisticated financial tools, Internet contacts and virtual data repositories, is that perhaps at last you can really obtain all the facts you need. Wrong. There is too much to analyse and by the time you finish the attempt, events have moved on. It is like trying to grab a handful of water from a running tap. The old Soviet Empire was a prime example of an organization that invested heavily in 'control'. Most of its bureaucracy was invested in knowing what went on (very little, as a direct consequence of all that control).

Organizational control at the higher level is structuring the organization to be sufficiently flexible to respond to the rapidly changing world. Control at the individual level is much the same – being flexible and skilful enough to figure out a course of action, guided by your values and goals, faced with a fluid and unpredictable world. Control of others is allowing them to carry out their work with adequate guidance and minimal interference.

Attending meetings, supervising paperwork, knowing what's going on in detail, does not give you control, it just keeps you busy. This is when you are least in control – you know everything about the car as it runs out of control downhill except how to stop it. There is one good pointer to whether you have an excess of this illusionary control. If you can answer most of the questions that land on your desk, then you are being paid to do other people's work. Those questions need to be answered further down the line, and this means giving away responsibility and demanding results. Also, by receiving these questions you are actually stopping the people from learning the answers themselves. Too much help disempowers as effectively as too little.

You are most in control when you are congruent in yourself about what you are doing, you have a clear direction, and your people are working unbeknownst to you, networking, taking initiatives, making decisions, achieving results and serving your customers. To do this they need your trust, and as much knowledge and information as they can handle.

Every action has consequences which can never be completely controlled because they can never be known for sure. However carefully you plan, the market is unpredictable, and success is often down to luck – being in the right place at the right time. This may be frustrating, but it will also create chances out of thin air. Small actions can have large consequences; the actions you take at an individual level can pay tremendous dividends. A word of encouragement can make the difference between a person giving up on a problem or giving it another day. Another day might result in a breakthrough that allows another team to advance its schedule by three months. Establishing a good relationship with a small customer may mean that they mention your name to their friend who works in a larger firm, who may then decide to give you an order. The quality of the relationship between a service provider and customer is a key factor in determining a customer's perception of the quality of the service he is receiving, in a market where the perceived quality of customer service is a big influence on product sales. This is systems thinking in practice. You can make a difference, but it may be in ways that seem surprising.

Relationship skills will be supremely important, especially establishing a relationship of trust. We have argued that organizations will devolve much more into networks of goal-focused, accountable, project teams. The people in these teams have to be empowered and given responsibility and accountability unless you want to spend your time dealing with micro problems and answering innumerable questions. You have to trust them. Without trust, employees will be constantly sceptical of any initiative. Information has to be freely available. Again this means trust. Without trust, information is not shared, people do not learn, and self-management and initiative from individuals and teams does not happen. Without trust, project partners, customers, suppliers and consultants will not be able to function.

You can't half trust. How can you create trust? Trust exists in the other person's eyes; it is created by your words and actions. You cannot force it, or make it simply by saying 'Trust me'. Management texts may stress the importance of trust but rarely say how you can create it between individuals. Trust is one link between individual action and organizational result and it is within your power to influence. How you can do this in practice is the domain of NLP.

PACING AND LEADING

Rapport is the word used in NLP to describe a relationship of trust and mutual influence and is the basis of all successful communication. Rapport comes first from acknowledging a person. In NLP this is known as pacing. The general principle of pacing is first to acknowledge the other, to understand and enter their reality, rather than demand they understand and enter yours. On the personal level, it is the ability to give the acknowledgement that each of us needs. You build a bridge towards understanding. The principle of pacing and leading works at every level: your people, your peers, customers, organization and the market you are in. Once you have paced, you can lead to something different; you have a relationship of mutual influence.

Influencing is not manipulating, it is a natural consequence of human interaction and wholly compatible with acting with integrity. People do not like to feel manipulated, but they are open to being influenced. Our professional success and our personal happiness depend in large measure on just how good we are at influencing others.

The best managers are not just technically competent, but good with people. They recognize how important it is that people feel acknowledged and address this fact in the way they behave. That a person feels acknowledged is much more important to them than mere agreement with their position. When a person feels acknowledged by you, they are quite likely to become a goodwill ambassador on your behalf. And as every advertising agency knows, there is no better form of publicity than an unsolicited endorsement from a disinterested third party.

PACING – ACKNOWLEDGEMENT

In order to motivate and manage people you need to know what is important to them as well as what is important to you. Recently we were working with a sales manager who had been singled out by his company as being particularly successful at motivating his people. Our brief was to model him to determine what specifically it was he did and said that made him so good. We would then install these skills in other managers in the company. This is the essence of 'modelling' as the word is used in NLP. One part of his success was really very simple. Whenever he wanted to motivate his staff, he would always begin by checking out how they were at the present time. Did they feel satisfied with this month's figures or were they a bit down about their performance? Sometimes he would explicitly ask them, other times he would take his cue from a person's overall posture and demeanour. In his words, 'Only when I know how they are can I know what they need and how to give it to them.' Another time he unwittingly summed up the art of pacing and leading: 'Of course I know where they need to go. But only when I know where they are now can I figure out how to get them to where they should be.'

To understand how pacing works, think of relay running. To pass on the baton, both runners must be going at the same pace. It is the job of the one who is taking over to pace the previous runner so that it can be handed over effortlessly without any stumbling or change of pace.

You can also pace people with your gestures and actions as much as with your words. When a colleague has had some good news, you would say, 'Congratulations!', but if you said it in a dull tone of voice and looked down slumping your shoulders, you would not be pacing them.

Pacing works because we are all different, we all have different models of the world built from our beliefs, values and life experiences. To be a truly effective communicator you need to respect that each person has their own way of looking at the world: you can say the same thing to different members of staff and obtain totally different results. Each person's model is not just an intellectual construct, it is a way of being which they will quite literally embody. The way a person breathes, the way they hold themselves, all are in part a function of how they perceive the world and their place in it. Someone who tends mostly to stoop and frown, for instance, is telling you something about how their internal world is structured and which is important for you to know – especially if they want you to hire them as an inspirational speaker!

Different cultures conduct themselves quite differently. Some of the most successful managers we have worked with instinctively adjust their behaviour quite unconsciously when in a different culture. This too is pacing.

You pace your customer base by finding out what they want, and then supplying it. No organization in its right mind would say, 'We don't care what you want, we are going to make this product so you are just going to have to buy it.' The most telling customer complaint is, 'You don't care.' A company with such a reputation is courting corporate death. On an individual level, salespeople pace customers by finding out their needs, and meeting them if they can. Some organizations have one rule for the customers and another for their staff. They see no discrepancy in being very attentive to the customer and very authoritarian to their staff. This usually goes with a hierarchical structure and a strong belief in being in control. Too often companies talk about 'quality' for their customers while giving a singularly unconvincing demonstration of it in the office in the way they handle their own people. There is something particularly odd about coming into contact with people who have been trained in customer care but who do not feel cared for themselves. Telling people what to do without first pacing them does not work. It produces a mixture of inertia and a kind of black market initiative where individual creativity goes on non-work related projects.

Organizations often make a basic mistake of not pacing enough, or leading without any pacing. A product launched without sufficient consultation, sufficient market research or sufficient preparation has much less chance of success. Similarly, organizational change is likely to work when it builds on past successes and takes into account the fears of the people who will have to change.

TIME AND (E)MOTION STUDIES

Many a management initiative is sabotaged by people who feel insufficiently consulted and acknowledged. In the initial days at Semco, management hired a consultancy to do time and motion studies to analyse the workers' routines. The intention was to help the workforce increase productivity. The study was sadly inconclusive. Much later, when trust had been established, the workers who had been the object of the study said that they had quickly learned how to slow down the analysts' timers to bias the results.

Pacing is not passively sitting back and reacting to other people or events. When a person is active and enthusiastic, you pace them by being active and enthusiastic in turn. When customers demand new products fast, you give them. You pace the current fast-changing, competitive global markets by being quick to learn and adjust, and to use the opportunities. This book will show you how to successfully pace and then lead the current business culture. Pacing is the means of achieving what you want on a individual or a corporate level. *Pacing is the means to be successful in any endeavour.* To do it you need to be flexible, because you never know what you may be called on to pace.

One of the arts of advertising is to pace a new product into an existing market, and how the agencies do it depends on the market. In a soft drinks market, where consumers are always on the lookout for something new to try, then a campaign that stresses newness and difference will pace that market. In a conservative market that is slow to change, then concentrating on how the new product will let the customers do what they have always done, only better, makes more sense.

LEADING – INFLUENCE

Once you are pacing, then you can think about the second step – leading. Leading is the ability to influence. Sometimes it is only a matter of pointing out the goal towards which you want to be heading. More often though it involves helping people to change their point of view, or anything else which is inhibiting their ability to allow you to do your job. Most people make the mistake of trying to lead before they have paced, of putting the cart before the horse.

The strategy for successful people management is constant and simple:

pace, pace, pace . . . lead.

The means of implementing leading are legion. One strategy, many tactics. They are the tools for successful managing and we will deal with many of them in the following pages.

Pacing and leading are the basic principles for influencing and managing people, and we will consider them in practice from many different angles throughout this book – organizational and personal, with self and others. Where to start? We suggest by pacing yourself. Acknowledge your own strengths, and where you need to learn. Know the conditions when you are at your best and when you are not. Respect your limits, your health and your degree of influence. Start from where you are. Then you can lead yourself to where you want to be.

We began this chapter with a quotation from *The Prince*, the bible of statecraft for centuries, by Machiavelli, who wrote in the sixteenth century for rulers of countries rather than organizations. Change is difficult, it calls for courage, yet the personal and professional rewards are great. The situation now is such that you have to change to survive. Remember the saying: There are three types of managers: those who make things happen, those who watch what happens and those who say, 'What happened?'

FURTHER READING

Jacob, Rahul, 'Managing, the Struggle to Create an Organisation for the 21st Century', *Fortune*, 3 April 1995.

Peters, Tom, *Liberation Management*, Pan Books 1992.

Senge, Peter, *The Fifth Discipline – The Art and Practice of the Learning Organisation*, Century Business 1990.

Semler, Ricardo, *Maverick!*, Century 1993.

NOTES

1   Machiavelli, N., *The Prince*, Penguin 1961.
2   Deegan, Paul, *Operation Desert Storm*, BBDO 1991.
3   Luthans, Fred, *Real Managers*, Ballinger Publishing Co. 1988.

2
RAPPORT

❖

Rapport is the relationship of trust and mutual influence that is at the heart of managing people. The key assets of an organization are its people. They are the imagination and the creativity of the organization, but they are not unchangeable. They are influenced by the weather, the office colour scheme, the air conditioning, whether they feel valued, and whether they had a fight with their spouse. They have 'moods'. Some days they are 'hot', some days they are not. They have individual character, ways of looking at the world based on their unique experience of life. Rapport is basically meeting individuals in their model of the world – pacing their reality. We have all had different upbringings, experiences and ways of being. We are all unique, with different values and skills. We each see the world differently. If you have rapport with someone they feel you understand how it is for them. In turn they will be much more accommodating to you and your needs. It does not mean that you have to agree with them. It is perfectly possible to maintain rapport with someone while overtly disagreeing with them. Conversely most people have experienced someone agreeing with them and finding it irritating. Agreement does not guarantee rapport.

The model of 'managing' by moving people round rather like chess pieces to accomplish your goals and checkmate the competitors was part of the old paradigm of large hierarchical organizations where everyone had their role to play. This old model still lingers on in some factory assembly lines where people are assigned small tasks with rigid job descriptions, and are watched by an overseer to ensure they stick to them. It is hard to think of a better way of disconnecting people from their work. Why should they care about what they do when they do not feel connected with the product of their labours? This factory model came from ideas of efficiency, breaking

17

work down into small components, and allocating a small task to each person so that they become very good at it. The new model of managing is more like what has always existed in the professions. Professionals have always worked on the principles of shared values, recognized competence, trust and flexibility. And they can still be very efficient. As more and more work is done by project teams, perhaps including outsiders, managers face a new challenge in dealing with them. Being able to build rapport with many different people becomes more and more important. Influencing people is central to managing, and managers work the magic to connect individuals to the organization.

Technology is increasingly replacing the repetitive, impersonal tasks in many areas of business, and not only in manufacturing industries. For example, neural network computers are being used in banking to make decisions about a customer's suitability for a loan, a task traditionally reserved for managers. Now, managers who presided over the automation of many clerical jobs in the banking industry are seeing the technology coming uncomfortably close. However, although computers do many tasks excellently, what they do not do is build relationships.

Building good relationships is one of the keys to being happy, feeling fulfilled and achieving our goals. Any enterprise that fosters these qualities in its people is much more likely to thrive. When we relate well, we feel real, valued, and understood. We connect with others while staying in touch with ourselves. In contrast, when we are not relating well, we tend either to lose ourselves, or become isolated in attempting to buttress our position. Being able to relate to your staff, your customers and your superiors is particularly important: it is the primary means you have of making your job easier, establishing your worth and enhancing your reputation as an individual *within* the organization. Creating a culture which supports such relating is a sound business move. And like charity, this begins at home, i.e. *within* the organization not just between the organization and its suppliers.

These skills of relating, communicating, and therefore influencing are pervasive. We are all involved in managing people, be it a company, a department, a family, a close relationship or simply ourselves. Similarly we are all involved in selling, be it a product, a vision, our competency and personality at an interview, or who we are, when we meet someone we find attractive at a party.

Until recently, having rapport was a rather haphazard affair. Some managers just seemed to have the knack and others didn't. It was one of those talents that you seemed to be born with, or not. It was hardly deemed something that you could *learn*. Yet rapport is a learnable skill, and it begins with pacing.

PACING THE CULTURE

Every individual, every organization and every culture has its own model of the world. Some you may understand and feel at home in; others will seem decidedly odd to you, but some people are at home there. Different countries certainly conduct business in different ways, and it is increasingly important to recognize and pace differences as business becomes more international. 'When in Rome . . . do as the Romans do.'

The ability to pace a culture is the beginning of successful management relationships, particularly in Japan. As the head of one Tokyo-based investment company put it, 'Relationships begin and develop over meals, drinks and games of golf. And a company without relationships cannot exist in Japan.'[1] You must find out all you can about the people you are going to meet and the customs of the country you are in. In Japan, for example, confrontation is avoided because it results in loss of face for one party. Deals are struck slowly. The Japanese generally will want many more meetings than English or American management to build the relationship and check that you can think long term. Trust is very important. A nod does not necessarily mean 'I agree' but 'I hear you'. Decisions tend to be reached by consensus rather than by one decision maker. There are many ways an unsuspecting Western manager could make a gaffe.

CHEATED OUT OF AN ARGUMENT

A colleague told us about the time he visited India. He and his friend Bill wanted to hire a taxi into town. He watched in disbelief while his friend spent over ten minutes haggling with the driver about the fare. He became more and more animated, showing anger and incredulity, as did the taxi driver. The episode ended with Bill shaking hands both with the driver and the onlookers who had gathered round the argument. Everyone was grinning. 'Why didn't you just pay the price at the beginning?' asked our colleague, 'We could afford it. We've just wasted a quarter of an hour.' 'Yes,' said Bill, 'but we would have greatly offended the driver. They pride themselves here on their bargaining powers. It is a very important part of their lives. He would have felt cheated.'

Matching the social environment of an organization or a different country is not simply a matter of corporate entertaining, however. Constant attention to detail before, during and after a sale has been achieved is also necessary to maintain rapport. The European or American style is to visit customers until they have signed the contract and then stop. In Japan, the business starts after the contract. You need to know the nature of the organization, become acquainted with many of the personnel in the company and consider the mind of the customer, not your own mind. Relationships are important in American and English business culture too, but they are expressed differently and are implicit rather than explicit.

John Mole's book *Mind Your Manners: Culture Clash in the European Single Market*[2] gives examples of the cultural differences within Europe. A meeting is a meeting. Right? Wrong. For the British and Dutch, meetings are much more exploratory, attempting to find a consensus. In France and Germany, the decisions may already have been made and the meeting is to communicate them, not negotiate about them. The French and Italians are different again. Although they may not overtly dissent, they may well work against the proposal in the background if they do not agree with it. Unanimous agreement is necessary and vote taking should be avoided unless you are assured that everyone will vote in favour. Similar differences in expectations can be found when considering agendas. All European managers expect to be presented with a prepared agenda, but only North Europeans will expect to keep to it.

There are differences too in body language. For example, taking off your jacket in England usually signals settling down to business; in Germany it is taken to mean you are just slacking. Large generalizations yes, but there is a simple message – expect the unexpected because individuals, organizations and cultures are operating from radically different maps of the world. Even if you never leave your native land, every organization has its own culture.

INDIVIDUAL RAPPORT

Rapport is created between individuals not so much by what is said but by the largely unconscious body language: postures, gestures and voice tones that people use. Words transfer information. Body language and voice tone carry relationship. You have probably been in a situation where someone is agreeing with you, but you do not really feel in rapport with them. There have been many studies, following the work by Professor Albert Mehrabian at the University of California in Los Angeles in 1981,[3] of the impact of body language and voice tone, on our perception of the trustworthiness of other people. If words and body language conflict, we nearly always take the non-verbal message as more significant, although of course we pay attention to the words. We may not know why we do not trust someone: it may be a vague feeling of unease, the other was 'shifty', or what they said 'did not ring true'. Body language and voice are very significant for building rapport and we shall concentrate on them in this chapter. We also of course build rapport with the words we speak, and this will be dealt with in detail in Chapter 9.

Clothes and appearance are an important part of body language, and may be a statement about organizational culture. At the beginning of the 1980s a great many talented computer programmers and designers were working in Silicon Valley in California. Steve Jobs and his colleagues were looking for people to work in his newly formed company, Apple Computers. Dress code in Silicon Valley was, and is, fairly lax, but some of the larger companies were demanding that their computer people wear suits and ties like everyone else. It was a poor management decision. There was no pacing of these computer whiz kids whose non-conformity, independence, playfulness and sense of identity were expressed in their casual dress code of jeans and trainers. Here was a classic example of formal procedure overriding the most important element – encouraging and harnessing the creativity and comfort of their people. If managers had taken the trouble to imagine how these people would respond, they would have left well alone. Instead they tried to fit round pegs into rigidly square holes. Many programmers left, and there was no shortage of other places to work. Many joined Steve Jobs at Apple, who of course was not stupid enough to try to manage such minutiae. The rest, as they say, is history – the birth and development of the Macintosh computer.

MATCHING BODY LANGUAGE

Rapport is built by matching the body language and voice tone of others. It shows how you 'pay attention' to others, that you acknowledge them and their model of the world. Next time you are in a meeting, or indeed any public place such as a restaurant, look around and notice the people talking together. Those that are in rapport will tend to share the same posture. The way they move and speak to each other will be like dancing; there is a rhythm to their movements and speech, a connection between them. Matching body language is a normal way to connect with others, so NLP is only making explicit what we do naturally. For example, we sit down to talk to someone who is sitting, and stand if they are standing. It feels awkward for both parties to do otherwise. There are also unspoken rules about personal space that vary from culture to culture, and we feel uncomfortable if they are breached without permission. We tend to match the amount of eye contact we have with people. It is intimidating to be stared at, but if you like steady eye contact, you will be wary of a person who is forever looking away.

Match some aspect of the other person's body language if you want to build rapport. At very least, stand if they stand, sit if they sit, give them the same amount of eye contact they give you. You can go further by matching the speed and general frequency of their hand gestures, or the angle of their head. You will often see this happen in meetings. One way of knowing whether a proposal is acceptable in a meeting is to watch if others match the body language of the proposer. Similarly, you will often be able to see who is the dominant force at a meeting. When he or she shifts position, it sends ripples of movement round the table shortly afterwards, as other people move to stay in rapport.

When you match posture, do not immediately change your body to match the other person's. Be natural. Your intention in body matching is to share and understand the other person's experience of the world. It is *not* mimicry. Mimicry is exact and immediate copying, and is not respectful. Friends do not mimic each other; they do not slavishly adjust their posture every time the other makes a move – and neither should you. People quickly notice mimicry and it loses rapport instantly. Dancers should complement each others' movements. They show their relationship through their movements. People have very different movement patterns, because people are very different. When you body match, you are showing the courtesy and the flexibility to adjust your style to accommodate theirs.

Breathing patterns are one aspect of body language that is normally outside people's awareness. If you want a lesson in the power of body matching, experiment by matching another person's breathing. It will give you invaluable information about what it feels like to be that person; when you start breathing like someone else, the world suddenly seems different because you are using your body in a very different way. You do not need to match every breath exactly; aim for a comfortable approximation that is not so different from your normal breathing pattern that it is obvious. If you find it difficult to track another person's breathing watch the rise and fall of their shoulders. Also people have to take a breath before they talk. You may find matching breathing is best done in a one-to-one situation like coaching or mentoring one of your people.

MATCHING VOICE

Matching voice tone is another way of establishing rapport. Different people speak very differently, even when saying the same words. Some speak loudly, some softly (volume). Some people speak faster than others (tempo). Some have a higher voice than others (pitch). Voice matching comes naturally. With soft spoken colleagues, we tend to moderate our voice. When there is a mismatch of voice tone, it often implies a power relationship, the louder voice dominating the softer one. A person's voice is an important part of their personality. (Imagine the effect of a managing director who habitually spoke in a high-pitched whine.) One of the first steps for an aspiring politician is to have some voice coaching. The best way to voice match is to match the volume and approximate speed of your companion's speech.

Voice matching is also very important on the telephone. Do this from the very first greeting, by matching the volume and speed of the other person's voice. As the conversation progresses, you can fine tune your matching. Again we do this to some extent anyway. Observe and listen to some of your colleagues when they talk on the telephone. Their voices will change depending on who they are talking to. Sometimes you can guess who they are talking to by how they speak – an interesting NLP parlour game.

Make sure the staff in your department learn and use voice matching on the telephone. It is the way to establish rapport with every caller. If you train personnel in telesales, teach them this skill. The best telesales people have a great flexibility and ability to gain rapport by voice matching. When you have a workforce trained to respond to the different voice styles of the customers in the course of the working day, the increase in revenue and goodwill is remarkable. *Successful Selling with NLP*[4] by Joseph O'Connor and Robin Prior gives more information on telephone sales skills and gaining rapport generally in a sales situation.

TALKING UP THE ROOM TEMPERATURE

A New York-based textile executive gave us a graphic example of the importance of voice quality at the time when he had been appointed to head his company's operations in North Carolina. He had been an outstanding manager in New York, and the board also felt that his easy-going style would be suitable in that part of the world. However, he was quite unprepared for the reception he received during the first meeting in his new post. He described it as 'cold civility' and it made him feel very uncomfortable. He said, 'I didn't quite know what I had done, it seemed like I had insulted them, certainly alienated them.' At this point he became very astute. He kept a low profile and just *listened.* That night he woke up at 3 am knowing what to do to make himself at home there. The next morning when he met his colleagues, he finished each sentence with a slight inflection. It still had a New York accent, but that inflection at the end was a signal to them that he was prepared to meet them in their way of being. The effect was immediate and dramatic: 'I felt like the room temperature went up 10 degrees.'

You may have to deal with people who are angry or upset. Voice matching is an excellent way to acknowledge their feelings without either becoming intimidated, or becoming involved in a shouting match. An angry person demands your attention whether you think the anger is justified or not. Trying to argue an angry person out of their feeling is very unlikely to work. They will feel their concern is being sidelined, and are likely to become even angrier. Anger is energy. Echo the energy and urgency of the person's voice, by matching slightly *below* their level of volume and speed – not at the same level, or you risk worsening the conflict. Pace and lead. Once you have paced them in this way, you may gradually lead them by lowering your own voice. If you have rapport, they will follow you. A calm, placating voice tone from the beginning rarely works; it is often interpreted as patronizing. Customer service staff need these voice matching skills, as they are often the first point of contact for angry customers.

You may be called on to manage people who are very different from you and from each other. Your department may contain staff who vary widely in age and experience. Some may have high levels of formal education, while others have little formal education but may be very shrewd. By using body and voice matching you can gain rapport and be comfortable with a very wide range of people.

CROSSOVER MATCHING

Matching is never exact, nor would you want it to be. It would intrude on the other's awareness and call attention to itself. With matching, a little goes a long way. Crossover matching is when you match indirectly. For example, when a person crosses their legs, you can cross your arms. When someone repeatedly nods their head, you respond by moving your hand in a similar rhythm. We had a good example of crossover matching when a young man sought Ian's advice about a job promotion prospect. He was one of three people his managing director used to call in when fired with imagination and wanting someone to discuss his new ideas with. It was clear that the managing director was about to select one of the three to become his full-time assistant. The young man very much wanted the job, but was not sure whether he was any more qualified than the other two. However, although he shared the managing director's enthusiasm, he did not know how to convey that. During those sessions his boss was given to pacing the floor and gesticulating, while the assistants sat, discussed and took notes.

Ian suggested to the young man that he took a notepad and a pencil to the meeting, and then as the director strode across the floor, crossover match by tapping out the rhythm of the stride on the notepad. This matched the director's energetic state in an unobtrusive way without interrupting his creative flow. The effect was dramatic. The young man started to feel that the boss was speaking directly to him, eye contact between them increased enormously during those meetings. The young man was offered the job. After a month in his new post the boss took him out for a meal and told him he had been chosen for the job because, 'I just felt you were on my wavelength'. Rapport is often intangible, yet can make a tremendous difference in business relationships.

Matching body language and voice tone to gain rapport is a good example of NLP taking a pattern that people use naturally, refining it and making it a learnable skill. It is a natural by-product of interest in, and paying attention to, another person. When you use body matching or voice matching consciously to gain rapport, beware of two traps. It may seem rather artificial at first and you may feel awkward. This is because you are becoming aware of something you were doing before unconsciously. The purpose is to be able to do it even better. It is like taking an advanced driving course when you drive well already. The instructor will make you see your driving skills in a fresh light. You become a better, more controlled driver. Secondly, body matching and voice matching will feel and look hollow and contrived if you use it in an attempt to influence people you have no interest in, and do not actually want to talk to.

WORDS – TRUST IS NOT INFORMATION

At last. Words. The most obvious part of the communication, but the least important for building trust and rapport. When words and body language clash, we nearly always follow the body language. Imagine someone saying 'I trust you' with a slight sneer and a quizzical tone, while leaning slightly backwards. Would you believe them? Words are good for giving information, but building trust requires much more. That said, you can use language to build relationships as well as giving information; by listening carefully to what people say and using the words that are important to them in your reply. People mark out words that are important to them by stressing them tonally, or by making a hand gesture, just as we *italicize* important words in print. Using the same words or phrases in your reply shows them you hear and respect their meaning. This is not the same as paraphrasing. Your paraphrase will not necessarily mean the same to the other person as their words, although it may to you. The words people use give a window into their world. For example a colleague might say, 'We need more *team spirit* in this group.' Now you have no idea what 'team spirit' means to her, but make sure you use the same phrase when you discuss it with her and encourage her to tell you what it means to her. This way, she does the work instead of you trying to mind read. You may then broaden out and use some qualifying words, but pace by using her word before leading somewhere else.

Respect what people say – literally. It seems so obvious, trite even, that the temptation is to agree and pass on quickly. Nothing controversial there. And yet when you pay close attention you will see instances every day of people not listening to others, and then demonstrating that they are not listening by paraphrasing in a way that changes the original meaning. People tell you what they value all the time, the words they choose are important, and if NLP has brought one realization to the area of communication skills, it is to respect what people say as a literal description of events in their world. Attending to these small details makes a big difference to relationships, which make an even bigger difference to how effectively you manage, and how effectively you are seen to manage.

BACKTRACKING

Backtracking expands matching important words: you reflect back the other person's concerns using the same key words and phrases. This is very important in sales. If your paraphrase has a significantly different meaning for the customer you will lose rapport and demonstrate to them that you were not listening. Backtracking and summarizing lets them know that you were listening, and paces what they want. Then you can go on to leading through discussion and negotiation. Backtracking is useful in meetings and negotiations. People are much more willing to listen to what *you* have to say, if they feel listened to themselves. We have seen many negotiations become unstuck because each party is busy putting their demands on the table and ignoring the other's concerns. The irony is that sometimes these parties are more in agreement than they realize, but they cannot connect. Whenever someone keeps making the same point like an endless tape loop, you know that, in their world, you are not listening to them. Let this be a cue to backtrack.

Backtracking is a good way of checking for agreement; it builds and demonstrates rapport and surfaces any misunderstandings. Has there been a time when a colleague has asked you to do something, and you thought you knew what they meant, went away and did it, only to find that you had misunderstood? This situation is annoying, and sometimes degenerates into blaming and bad feeling:

> 'You should have understood.'
> 'Well I would have done if only you had been clearer.'

When you backtrack you can check your understanding by asking questions. Backtracking also acts as a punctuation in a meeting. Summarizing what has gone before establishes a shared agreement and a platform from which to move on. It will bring up any disagreements sooner rather than later.

It might seem artificial to repeat what another person has just said. You may think they will be offended in some way. Very unlikely. Of course if you simply parrot what they say back to them without the body language that tells them you are involved and engaged, then yes, they may be offended. However, if you are building rapport, most people will be profoundly relieved that here at last is someone who is taking the trouble to listen to them, taking what they say seriously and checking back with them.

MISMATCHING

Matching is joining someone in their particular dance. Mismatching is deliberately stepping out of the dance, without losing rapport. Some forms of mismatching will lose rapport – turning your back, looking at your watch and sighing are some rather crass examples of mismatching. Given the power of matching to establish rapport, mismatching is a very necessary skill. It allows you to terminate a meeting at your discretion. Do you want to extricate yourself from a conversation without appearing rude? Mismatch body language. Looking away, increasing the rate of head nodding are some actions you will see, and may have used.

Mismatching is also a method of disengaging for a moment to give the other person a chance to think over a suggestion. A good way is to physically increase the distance between the two of you. It literally gives them space to think. Mismatching voice tone is a good way to end a telephone conversation without appearing rude (a very useful skill). Some people do not accept the message when you say you have to go. Mismatch voice tone. Talk faster and louder, while saying the appropriate words of farewell. The caller receives both a verbal and non-verbal message. The better the previous rapport, the more effective is the mismatch.

Mismatching can also be a communication in its own right. One executive told us that when he joined a new company he felt that his people were too subservient. 'We had these general meetings and they would keep addressing their comments and observations to me rather than to each other.' He decided he would start to mismatch the individuals who were particularly prone to doing this. 'I started by avoiding eye contact, then I began to look out of the window. When this didn't work, I got up and left the room telling them to carry on. When I returned and sat down they were finally talking to each other.'

OGRES AND ICONS

You can consistently create rapport with a wide variety of people using body and voice matching. The manager's role in the organization is independent of his personal skills, but these skills will make his role much easier to perform satisfactorily. Many management courses neglect this personal dimension and concentrate on the ability to perform tasks. There is also the question of degree of rapport between individual managers and their role in the organization. Many senior managers have their capability and sense of self hindered and influenced by the expectations of their juniors. Thus they become trapped by organizational beliefs and may even finish acting out a part written for them by others. Junior managers create ogres and icons of their seniors. They then react to the ogre or the icon of their own creation and it is hard for the real person to disentangle their identity from the icon. Expectations and issues concerning gender roles also come into play. Women are often trapped by rigid expectations of how they ought to behave, and lose part of themselves in order to function at work.

When you are working with people pace their role: manager, overseer, boss, receptionist, whatever it may be, and avoid simplistic expectations. There is a real person in the role. Pacing the role does not establish any personal contact, and without personal rapport there will be no bond beyond the execution of the present task.

The strongest rapport comes from acknowledging the person's identity. When a person feels acknowledged at this level, they are open to being influenced. There are tell tale expressions which people will use when they are asserting their identity, be it personal or organizational. The most common are, 'I'm not that kind of person,' or 'We're not that kind of organization.' When people say things like that they are letting you know that they clearly do have a sense of self and what someone has said or done potentially violates it. It is not an irretrievable situation, but you need to respond to it immediately. If it is something you said it is important to determine what it was. The most successful way of pacing the identity of another is very simple. Allow them to be who they are. It is hard to do if you cannot do it for yourself.

This means being who *you* are. You are in rapport with yourself because you are pacing your own identity. In NLP it is known as being *congruent*, and it is a recurring theme in this book.

Body matching is not sufficient for rapport if you mismatch values and beliefs. Pacing a person's values and beliefs does not mean you have to agree with them. One of the most fundamental errors in communication is to assume that the beliefs and values we hold are shared by others and to act accordingly. So many people go through life giving what they most want to receive, rather than what the other person wants and, equally, receiving what the other person most needs, but which they themselves do not want. To step off this particular carousel, you have to remember everyone has their own individual map of reality. Understand their map, rather than giving them yours.

A colleague of ours recently began working on an important project with another manager who was busy preparing a paper which he was due to present in a couple of months time. He had thought of a great title for the paper, but was having problems organizing his material. The deadline was looming and the paper began to occupy more and more of his waking thoughts. As a result their meetings began to take a particular form. He would come in, and before they could start work on the project, he would let off steam about his problem paper. Our colleague was one of the few people he could talk to about it. Recognizing that it was important for him to have that time, she decided to budget fifteen minutes per meeting, at the beginning, to do nothing else but to talk about his paper. Fifteen minutes is a long time, but it was a sound investment; as a result he felt well and truly matched. It built a high level of trust, and now the project is under way, they are working well together.

RAPPORT WITH CUSTOMERS

Many purchase and repeat purchase decisions are influenced by relationships. More and more firms are paying attention to building relationships with customers through different means such as customer clubs, magazines, and competitions. Rather than bombarding the market with advertising, consumer goods marketers often have two distinct advertising budgets – one for gaining new customers and the other for keeping existing ones. Lifetime customers are worth money, not only the money they spend, but also the good word-of-mouth advertising they do. As a client of ours put it, 'If I really like your product I might create half a dozen other lifetime customers for you.' A single customer walking through the door for the first time might be potentially worth hundreds of thousands of pounds. A good enough reason for establishing rapport!

Sales people need to be able to build rapport with customers. In a competitive market where there is little difference in prices and products, the salesperson is the difference that can make a difference.

The Forum Corporation have extensively researched customer loyalty, summarized in *The Customer-Driven Company* by Richard Whiteley.[5] A survey was taken of the former customers of fourteen companies from both the manufacturing and service sectors of business. The survey found that 15 per cent of the customers switched to another company because they 'found a better product'. There were 15 per cent who switched because they 'found a cheaper product'. So 30 per cent switched because of price or traditionally defined quality. Another 20 per cent switched because of 'too little contact and individual attention'. Nearly 50 per cent switched company because 'the attention they received was poor in quality', which means that over two-thirds switched because of how they felt about the relationship. Quality and price are important, but people make relationships. Rapport skills are necessary for all staff who deal with customers. When companies start investing in relationships, the return can be phenomenal.

DEVELOPING YOUR SKILLS

These various skills are most easily learnt one at a time, but used best in conjunction with each other. None of them in isolation guarantees rapport. You might match someone at behavioural level with posture and gesture, but mismatch values and lose rapport. On the other hand if you only match their values, you may never achieve that real rapport that comes from feeling comfortable with someone. These skills are designed to enable you to establish and maintain rapport rapidly within minutes of meeting. Rapport develops and strengthens over time. It is the exact opposite of pretence, which decays over time.

MATCHING BODY LANGUAGE

○ Study those colleagues who have good rapport skills. What do they do? Are they body and voice matching?

○ Watch the body language of colleagues as they talk in meetings and general conversations. Do they match body language? Observe strangers talking. Go 'people watching'. Do they match body language? Could you tell which people are getting on well in their conversation by observing their body language, and without hearing their words?

○ Match the amount of eye contact used by colleagues and customers. If they give a lot of eye contact, give the same amount in return. If they are sparing, be sparing too.

○ In low risk situations, take a moment to notice how much you are matching the other person. Respectfully start matching another person's body postures, movement style and gestures. Do this with people you feel comfortable with. As you become more skilled, you will be able to build rapport in this way with very different people, even those with whom you were initially ill-at-ease. Notice the difference this makes to the conversation.

○ Experiment by mismatching body language. From a matching position, change posture, gesture, balance and amount of eye contact. Does it affect the flow of the conversation? Caution – this can make people very uncomfortable if you persist. Go back to matching afterwards.

VOICE MATCHING

○ Notice how colleagues' voices change when they are talking to different people on the telephone. Can you guess who they are talking to?

○ Experiment by matching the volume of the people you talk to on the telephone. Do the calls flow more smoothly? When you feel comfortable matching, pick an easy call and once you have rapport, start to change the tempo of your voice. Does your telephone partner follow? If so, you have good rapport, and you have paced

his voice and then been able to lead. If he does not, go back to
pacing.

○   Try mismatching volume and speed at the end of a call. Decide
    when you want the conversation to end and speed up your voice
    and speak slightly louder. Listen to whether the other person
    follows and terminates the conversation. If they do not, then you
    can use words like, 'I must be going now, speak to you later . . .
    etc.'

○   When you are comfortable matching voice tone from telephone
    conversations, match volume and speed of voice with friends and
    colleagues in face-to-face conversations. Use low-risk meetings at
    first. Begin by matching volume. When you are comfortable with
    this, continue by matching speed and rhythm. Notice the effect this
    has on the conversation.

BACKTRACKING

○   The next time you are talking to a colleague and you want
    something that is important to you, notice if he or she uses your
    same important words back to you. How do you feel in each
    case?

○   When you are meeting a colleague who wants something, back-
    track what they say using their key words, then start to discuss their
    demand.

CULTURE

○   Make a mental note of at least three differences that characterize
    the culture of every organization you go into. Compare your notes
    with colleagues to see if they have the same impressions.

FURTHER READING

O'Connor, Joseph, and McDermott, Ian, *Principles of NLP*, Thorsons 1996.

NOTES

1   Ferguson, Anne, 'Playing the game the Japanese way', *Independent on
    Sunday*, 22 April 1990.
2   Mole, John, *Mind Your Manners: Culture Clash in the European Single
    Market*, Corgi 1990.

3 Mehrabian, A., *Silent Messages*, Wadsworth 1971.
4 O'Connor, Joseph, and Prior, Robin, *Successful Selling with NLP*, Thorsons 1995.
5 Whiteley, Richard, *The Customer-Driven Company*, Addison Wesley 1991.

3
POINTS OF VIEW

❖

Telling someone to leave is probably the most unpleasant task faced by any manager. Employees tend to judge a company by how it conducts sackings or redundancies. It is the same in your private life. When the going is tough, you find people often show their true colours. When asking people to leave is done badly, good people start to leave soon afterwards. There are many horror stories of poorly handled sackings and lay-offs. People have been taken out to lunch and fired between the soup and main course. Sometimes there is an announcement of redundancies followed by an anxious wait for those who may be affected. Friday afternoon is a popular time to pass on the bad news. Most poor practice is the result of not being able to imagine what it's like to be in the other person's shoes.

THE BLACK SACK

A national newspaper became infamous for the way it sacked journalists – the 'black binliner job'. After the unfortunate person was notified, he would be taken back to his desk by security guards and given a black binliner. He had to transfer the contents of his desk into the binliner under scrutiny and would then be escorted from the premises.

The ability to understand another person's point of view is a basic skill in managing people. You flinch at the thought of being sacked in so cavalier a fashion because you are able to identify with the person on the receiving end.

PERCEPTUAL POSITIONS

The art of seeing events through the eyes of others is the skill embodied in the NLP idea of perceptual positions. Being able to look into the mind of your opponent has long been recognized as the mark of a master strategist, whether a corporate CEO or a chess grandmaster. It is also the reason Field Marshal Montgomery kept a photograph of the enemy Commander Rommel beside him during the desert war. Even when we are in opposition to someone it is important to be flexible enough to walk an imaginary mile in their shoes. Not because we agree with them, but to know how they will react.

One of the great contributions that NLP has made to communications research is to pay attention to what people actually say, their exact words, and respect their meaning. People talk of needing a 'different perspective', or looking at it from the 'company's point of view'. In NLP, these words are often taken literally, so a perceptual position is the perception you have from the position you have adopted. The place from which you perceive a situation affects what you can know. This can be true physically. Imagine two people negotiating, opposite each other, eyeball to eyeball. Literally opposite viewpoints. Now imagine those same people sitting side by side sharing a view of the flipchart depicting a shared problem. Which is more likely to foster the emergence of a 'common viewpoint'?

THE THREE POINTS OF VIEW IN NLP

NLP distinguishes between three main perceptual positions:

First position. Looking at the world from your own point of view. You have your own thoughts and feelings and you know what they are. When people say things like, 'Well, as far as I'm concerned . . .' you are getting their first position view.

Second position. Looking at the world from another person's point of view, perhaps a team member, boss, customer, supplier or competitor. When you say, 'If I were in your shoes . . .' you are taking second position as long as you actually try on their way of doing things.

Third position. Seeing both the former points of view, and the relationship between them, a wide, systemic view. This is also the world of the skilled negotiator and mediator, who usually start in first position picking up whatever impression strikes them. Then they go to second position to find out what it looks like to each of the parties concerned. Then they take up a third position where they can look at the situation in a detached way, receiving a rounded perspective. This third position incorporates all they know from the viewpoints of both parties, but is different from any of them. It is rather like the way our eyes work. Using the right eye gives one view. Using the left eye gives a second, different view. Both are two dimensional. Using both together gives three-dimensional vision (see Figure 3.1).

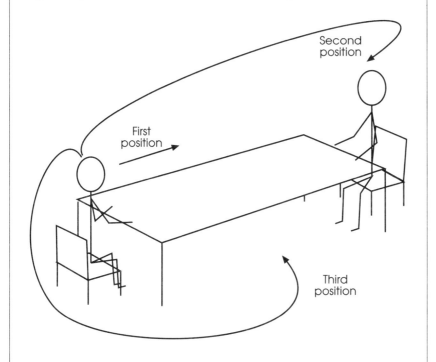

FIGURE 3.1   THREE-DIMENSIONAL VISION

NLP offers a systematic way of training people to perceive things from different positions. Good trainers and presenters, for example, have become very skilled at it. They know what they want to say. They picture what they look like from the audience's point of view. They imagine what it is like to be in the audience looking at and listening to themselves on stage. Then they imagine they are off to the side, looking at the presenter (themselves) and the audience and gauging the chemistry between the two. This is the viewpoint of the video camera. Some trainers do not learn very much from seeing themselves on video because they are too busy experiencing first position feelings of inadequacy and embarrassment (or pride), as they view the video. Third position should be both resourceful and engaged, yet detached from first position feelings. Good trainers literally adjust their presentation all the time based on their real time feedback from being able to see the presentation from different points of view. They can embody that famous definition of leadership: 'the ability to change the second half of your sentence based on the feedback you receive to the first half'.

There is a salutary tale of the danger of not taking second position in the book, *Interstate Commerce: Regional Styles of Doing Business.*[1] Three executives from Los Angeles went to make a presentation to a company in Knoxville, Tennessee, about the manufacture and sale of goods at a big convention to be held there. The Los Angeles group began their presentation by talking about how profitable the deal would be. They gave facts and figures. The executives from Knoxville looked embarrassed, and the presenter, misunderstanding what he saw, held out hope of even greater profits. The other two parts of the presentation about the quality of the items and the sales outlets were well received. The leader closed the presentation by returning to the subject of profits, and his audience again looked uncomfortable.

The Los Angeles group failed in their bid for the order. The reason only became clear later. To the Knoxville group, profits were taken for granted, and certainly not publicly discussed. They were a necessary part of the deal, but to be kept in the background. The Californian approach seemed brutally direct to them, as if profit was the main motive to be discussed. They did not want this. What could the Los Angeles group learn from this? First, perhaps the value of knowing how business is conducted in different parts of America, and pacing their hosts. Secondly, to remember that when you are in a hole, stop digging!

> 'When a salesman goes on holiday, take his place.'
> Peter Drucker

KNOW YOUR BIAS

The ability to take another person's point of view, that is, to take second position, becomes a liability if you do it too much and lose touch with what is important to you – your first position. It is possible to be too understanding. More commonly in business, however, people find it difficult to go to second position. This is not because they do not know how to. Anyone who has been scared, excited or moved by a film has gone to second position with the characters on the screen. It is a matter of being able to do so at will and having the will to do so. One reason why people may lack the will is that they are afraid of becoming too understanding and so undermine their own position, or they do not have a strong enough sense of themselves, and fear they will lose their own view. We have worked with senior managers and some CEOs who have had these fears. The greater the fear, the more bluff and bravado. They develop an autocratic management style that is untenable in the long run because other people show their dissatisfaction and leave the company.

A third position view will show you if you lean too far towards first or second position. Too many managers never step back and allow themselves another viewpoint, either of a situation, or their response to that situation. Taking different points of view is the way to think strategically, both at the individual and at the organizational level; the alternative is endless fire fighting.

A client of Ian's, a director of a large advertising concern, was having difficulty in dealing with two of his assistants. He had done his best to explain the changes he wanted to make. 'I bent over backwards to be reasonable with them,' he said. During an extended coffee break, Ian invited him to physically step out of the place where he had been describing these problems and take a fresh perspective. From this third position, he imagined looking at himself being reasonable. Ian asked him how he reacted to what he was doing in that stuck situation. He became red and flushed. 'I feel very angry with him,' pointing to where he had been a moment before, being so very reasonable. He then walked back to first position taking that anger with him, and Ian asked him what he thought would be the best thing to say now to his subordinates. Without a moment's hesitation he replied, 'There need to be some big changes round here and I need you to make them. If you don't make them by the end of the week, we are going to have to sit down and review your contract!' Later that day he had a meeting with them. As he described it afterwards, he was surprised at his own forcefulness, and yet they did not seem to take it amiss at all. Indeed one of them later told a colleague that she had been thinking of leaving because she felt she was not receiving strong direction from her boss. This is a variation on the theme of switching positions to obtain more knowledge and a broader view.

If you always do what you have always done, you will always get what you
have always got.

In some stuck situations involving other people, it sometimes seems
we are
powerless – we cannot make them change, even though we are
sure it is
necessary and best for everybody.
You do have some power.
You have control of one part of the situation – yourself.
Change your reaction and others involved will have to change as
well.
Changing perceptual positions is one way to do this.

THE MYTH OF THE RIGHT ANSWER

Taking first, second and third position is one way of learning to understand
yourself, your colleagues, your boss, your customers and your organization.
Management is such a broad subject that many views are possible. Market
strategy may point in one direction, customer feedback in another.
Management gurus give conflicting opinions. You need all the views you
can obtain. Some managers are reluctant, believing either they will get
confused, or one view has to be 'right' which means the others are 'wrong'.
This kind of thinking is a trap. The view of a building from the front is no
more right than the view from the back. If you want a full picture, you need
both.

There is a good story of Alfred Sloan, when he was president of General
Motors. At a top committee meeting a unanimous decision was reached,
whereupon Sloan said, 'I propose we postpone discussion on this matter
until our next meeting when we will have had time to develop some
disagreement and so understand this matter better.'

'The test of a first class mind is the ability to hold two opposing ideas
at the same time and still have the ability to function.'
Scott Fitzgerald

THE CUSTOMER VIEWPOINT

A manager will see the company from the inside, sliced up into departments and levels of responsibility. The customer sees the company as one unit. External customers perceive an organization horizontally, not vertically. Customers will complain about faulty goods and return them. They do not know or care whether it was due to a design fault or a breakdown in the quality procedures at a factory five hundred miles away. They want a replacement that works. A multinational telephone company for example has many different departments, some not even in the same country. Customers experience one company whether they are dealing with an operator, an engineer, a new installation or a maintenance contract. And they will complain centrally when something goes wrong. Thus a whole organization can have an undeserved reputation in its customers' eyes if one small department makes a mistake. It does work the other way, however. A customer's good experience with one part of the company, reflects on the whole business.

Your perspective on a problem may make it hard to find a solution. For example, here is a puzzle. Your task is to join all nine dots with four connecting straight lines without lifting your pencil from the paper:

```
    o   o   o

    o   o   o

    o   o   o
```

Clue: If you stay within the area bounded by the dots, the problem is unsolvable. Use the space outside the box bounded by the dots.

Here's an added twist. Can you join those nine dots with only three connecting straight lines? To do this you need a still wider per-spective.   A problem may only be a problem because of the confined space within which we are searching for a solution.

(For solution, see Figure 3.3 p. 55.)

FLOATING VIEWPOINTS

A good example of the havoc and expense that can be incurred when different perspectives are not taken into account is the 'pentium floating point' fiasco. The pentium microprocessor ('computer chip') was the first of a new generation of faster chips made by Intel. Motorola, their main competitor, had also launched a new chip. The market was volatile and undefined; the fortunes of hardware manufacturers such as IBM and Apple were also linked to the success of the competing microprocessors which form the heart of the computer hardware.

The pentium chip had a 'bug'. Intel had known about it for some time, but had treated it as a technical problem. They had taken an engineering perspective rather than a customer–public relations one, despite the fact that they had gone a long way in previous years towards recreating themselves as a marketing company. A computer chip is not very interesting in itself, but the 'power at the heart of your business' certainly is, and their slogan 'Intel inside' was a clever statement of this. Intel decided that as the bug was such a small fault and statistically almost negligible, they did not have to worry about it, and therefore neither would their customers. Wrong! When the problem publicly came to light, Intel issued a statement that basic spreadsheet users would hit an error once every 27,000 years. This was absolutely accurate but did little to allay customer disquiet.

Intel competitors were not slow to point out that the risk would be greatly increased for a financial analyst who uses spreadsheets most of the day, and this is precisely the person who cannot afford to make an error. Also, normal users do not use the random floating point values that Intel used to illustrate the possibility of error. They use other calculations that would increase the chance of a mistake. Intel had analysed the statistics, but did nothing to calm the fears of the customers, who were uninterested in statistical analyses or the theoretical chances of error. Their perception was that of a car owner who finds out there is a design fault in the engine that means there is a risk of a crash – a totally unacceptable situation. A survey in the USA at the time quoted the average consumer comment: 'I am not sure what a Pentium is, but I know something is wrong with it.' Bad news for Intel, who to their public relations credit, but accounting debit, set about recalling and replacing all faulty chips.

Here, we write that 'Intel' did this or that. Organizations do not of course take decisions, people decide. In the case of Intel, the decision makers might have taken another course if they had asked themselves such questions as: 'How will this look from a customer point of view?' 'How does this look from an engineering point of view?' 'How will this look from a hardware manufacturer's point of view?' 'How might my competitors use this?' Simple questions, expensive consequences. To do this they needed to 'become' the customer, engineer, hardware manufacturer, and competitor.

LOGICAL LEVELS

You can gather different perspectives not only from different people, but also at different levels. Some years ago Ian had the striking experience of working for two quite unrelated clients and hearing similar words offered by employees of each to explain why things were going awry.

In the first case, a large financial services company was trying to persuade its telephonists not merely to take enquiries but to begin selling its services to the callers. They were meeting considerable resistance and when Ian talked to these people, he heard the same words over and over: 'That's not what *we* do.' It was as if they were personally affronted by the new management directive. What seemed to management like a simple change appeared as a fundamental redefinition of work to the staff who answered the telephones, from service to selling. They saw not only their role, but also who they were, being redefined.

The second client was a promotional company at loggerheads with its American parent company. The dispute was quite simple. The American parent wanted certain hard-selling practices that had worked well in the States to be instituted by the British offshoot. However, although the directors were willing to comply, the salespeople were not and the message that was coming back was, 'We can't do that *here*'.

The proposals were similar but the dilemma for each company was different. In the first case, people were responding to what they perceived as a threat to their identity. They were being required to change what they did. And what they did contributed to their sense of who they were within the organization. In the second case, people were not objecting to the activity, the hard sell, itself. Rather they were saying that activity was not acceptable in a particular context, namely the British environment.

The management made little headway in either case. They could not resolve the impasse because they did not appreciate the true issues they were dealing with. The financial services company failed to recognize that it had to reassure its people that their identity was not undermined. What was needed was a little pacing and then leading to a new job description. Instead, the failure to pace employees at the level of identity meant that they were quite intransigent when it came to changing their behaviour. A similar lack of pacing was evident in the promotional company. The salespeople were not disputing the effectiveness of the hard-sell techniques, but their relevance to the UK environment. (They were right. Management insisted, and a few years later the UK subsidiary was shut down, even though business in America was booming.)

These are examples of two different levels. NLP researcher and developer Robert Dilts offers an invaluable description of what individuals and companies do in terms of a series of levels (see Figure 3.2):

The first level is the *Environment (the where and the when)*
The environment is the place where we are and the people we are with. The comfort and the safety of your surroundings make a big difference to how well you work and how satisfied you are. People also use their environment to express their identity. An 'impersonal' environment is intimidating because there is no sense of the individual people who use it. The people who work there may set great store on their small personal belongings as a way of expressing their identity. Our co-workers are a very important part of the environment we work in. We will tolerate very poor physical environments provided we get on well with our work colleagues. It is very difficult to work in an environment without rapport with colleagues. Good relationships are as important as, or even more important than, ergonomic furniture and good air conditioning. And there is no equivalent of the Environmental Health Officer to fix rapport.

The second level is *Behaviour (the what)*
Behaviour is what we do. Examples of organizational behaviours are takeovers, advertising campaigns, restructuring and share offers. Individual

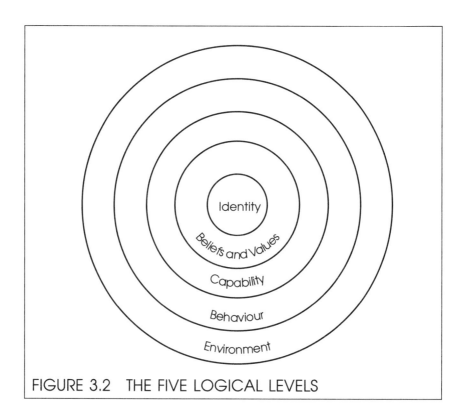

FIGURE 3.2   THE FIVE LOGICAL LEVELS

behaviour could be letter writing, decision making, or interviewing. Behaviour is the level of single actions.

The third level is *Capability (the how)*
Capability implies skill; organizations may attempt restructuring, but fail because they lack the capability. On the individual level, capabilities are those behaviours that we have practised so often they have become consistent, automatic and often habitual. When people talk about being able or skilful, they are usually talking about capabilities. Repeatable management processes are also at the capability level, as are appraising, and mentoring. Capability implies strategy, a way of working that achieves results; it supplies competence to existing confidence. When someone describes their success as a 'one-off' or a 'fluke', they are ascribing it to the level of behaviour only. They do not think it is repeatable consistently, it is not yet a capability. Managing is a capability, and one we are exploring widely in this book. In doing so we will touch on all the other levels both personal and organizational.

The fourth level is *Beliefs and Values (the why)*
This is the level of what we believe to be true and what is important. Organizational beliefs are often expressed in a mission statement, or articulated by senior managers. Belief statements can be framed in different ways. Sometimes they are 'if . . . then' statements. For example, 'If we change to a more open plan office, then we will not get so much work done' is a statement of belief. The words 'can' and 'can't' often hide beliefs, as they refer to what is thought possible, e.g. 'You can't achieve an increase in productivity with only half the staff.'

Values are what is important, why we act as we do. Organizational values are sometimes expressed in a mission or vision statement. Values are made real in action, and sometimes organizational behaviour is at odds with expressed views. There is much talk about people being a company's greatest asset, and how important it is to look after them. Yet those same companies may routinely expect people to sacrifice other parts of their life for their work, pay insufficient attention to providing a pleasant environment, and not trust them to make decisions. It is not what you say, but what you do that speaks loudest. When fixed procedures and rules disappear, so shared beliefs and values become the glue that holds organizations together.

The fifth level is *Identity (the who)*
Companies develop an identity, given time, which is often driven by the ethos and values of the founders. Richard Branson and Virgin is a good example. On an individual level, identity is your sense of yourself, your core beliefs and values that define who you are and your mission in life. Your

identity is very resilient, although you can build, develop and change it. Work provides one important opportunity to develop your identity.

THE LANGUAGE OF LEVELS

The structure of an organization emerges from these five levels – its offices and where it is situated, what it does, what it is capable of doing, what is important to it and its identity, or culture. Management problems can occur at any level. Some problems are intractable as long as they are being addressed at the wrong level. How do you know which level to address? One way is to listen to the exact words people use when describing their concerns, and not only the words, but the emphasis they give the words.

Suppose someone says to you, 'I can't do that *here*'. Clearly what he is telling you is not that he can't do it but that he can't do it in this particular environment. On the other hand, supposing he says '*I* can't do that here'. What he is telling you is not that it can't be done here, but that *he* can't do it here. You may well have heard somebody say 'I *can't* do that here'. A different message again. They are telling you about a belief they have. They are saying they do not believe they are able to do it.

We can map out all five logical levels using this same sentence:

IDENTITY	'*I* can't do that here.'
BELIEF	'I *can't* do that here.'
CAPABILITY	'I can't *do* that here.'
BEHAVIOUR	'I can't do *that* here.'
ENVIRONMENT	'I can't do that *here*.'

Examples of logical levels in speech:

Identity	I am a good manager
Belief	Taking the MBA helped me greatly.
Capability	I have excellent communication skills.
Behaviour	I did poorly in that appraisal.
Environment	The team works well here.
Identity	I am an entrepreneur.
Belief	Business should be allowed to maximize profit without interference from the government.
Capability	I delegate well to achieve results.
Behaviour	I expect you to be on time for our next meeting.
Environment	This open-plan office has improved communication.
Identity	We are not the sort of company that would use that appraisal system.
Belief	It's not important to be able to do that.

Capability	We are not in a position to implement that decision yet.
Behaviour	You handled that appraisal well.
Environment	The interview room was cold.

Here is an example from personal and family life:

Identity	You are selfish.
Belief	I can't have what I want.
Capability	I am very good at cooking.
Behaviour	Let's visit my parents.
Environment	Why don't you keep this room tidy?

Identity statements invariably involve 'I am', 'You are', or 'We are' phrases. They claim qualities for the person or organization. They can work for good or for ill. For example, 'We are a good team', is likely to be motivating and positive. 'You are a poor worker' is strongly negative. 'You found that task difficult' puts the difficulty at the level of behaviour and is much easier for the person to deal with. Behaviours can be changed and capabilities can be learned. That means there is hope and where there is hope people begin to take action. Identity statements tend to stick; most people believe that it is very difficult to change their identity and do not want to anyway.

As you begin to hear logical level statements, pick out what level someone is at and then pace them at that level before going any further. You may find it useful to lead them to another level, but first you must meet them where they are. So if someone complains about the environment and co-workers, acknowledge that first. Let them know you understand they have a problem at the environmental level. Then perhaps you might lead them to dealing with it by developing a capability. You could stay with the problem on the environmental level (for example, 'We will move you to another part of the building'). If a person is having trouble learning a procedure (capability) acknowledge that. You could address it at that level (training), or perhaps explore values – if they do not think the skill sufficiently important to learn, for example, then all the training in the world will not make any difference.

TALKING AT THE RIGHT LEVEL

Logical levels are a tool of organizational analysis, and you will find an immediate and obvious application in working with your people. They will tell you by the words they use at what logical level they are operating, and you can adjust your language to respond accordingly.

If you have positive statements to make to any of your people (or yourself), consider making them at an identity level, for example, '*You* are a great account handler'. When you have negative feedback for people give it at a behavioural level. If you give it in a negative form at an identity level you risk offending the person. Suppose you want people to do follow-up calls more quickly. Tell them, 'It's important to make a follow-up call within 24 hours always. You must do this in future.' In this way you are correcting the behaviour, not the person.

Levels can become confused all too easily. The single most common example is taking criticism about behaviour at the level of identity. That is to say, a criticism of their behaviour becomes a criticism of who they are, at least as far as they are concerned. Ian was working with the managing director of a direct marketing company who had built the business, was extremely dynamic, wanted to encourage creativity in his people and had instituted brain-storming sessions. But when people began to evaluate ideas afterwards, he was super sensitive if any of his were criticized. The effect was that people started to hold back in the brain-storming sessions and he could not understand why.

The remedy was to teach his people how to separate their criticism of his proposal from his identity. This involved a very simple two-part delivery format. First, affirm his identity by reinforcing his role (e.g. 'You are very good in this field'). Second, state your reservation (e.g. 'But I do not think that this particular approach will get us the best response'). It gave people a way of addressing him and separating his identity from his suggestion, which in turn allowed him to do the same. In effect they were teaching him how to make this separation by doing it for him. The result was remarkable. He became open to what people had to say, and in the process they had learnt to become more assertive. It was an empowering experience for them and they were able to become more dynamic and creative as a result.

IDENTITY CONFUSIONS

People often confuse their role with their identity. It is an interesting phenomenon that in our culture when you ask somebody, 'What do you do?' (i.e. behaviour or capability), people invariably respond with a statement that begins, 'I am a . . .'. That is to say, they respond at an identity level by telling you their job role. For many this role is a key, if not the central element in their identity, both in and outside work. It is why unemployment or dismissal can be so devastating. Your sense of self, your way of knowing who you are, has been taken away from you. So it is important not to confuse your professional role with your identity.

It is equally important not to confuse your behaviour with your identity. First-line managers in particular like to be liked. If their role is criticized, they often see this as an identity level criticism, instead of a criticism of behaviour.

Do not confuse your behaviour or identity with the identity of the organization. This is a trap for senior managers who, if criticized, may become affronted, because to them you are not criticizing their behaviour, you are criticizing the identity of the organization they represent. In all of these three cases the individual's identity is entangled with the behaviour, role, or organization they see themselves as personifying.

That said, a clear identity is important for both individuals and organizations because it is also the source of vision. If you do not know who you are, it is very hard to know what you want. It is also very difficult to see where you are going and to lead others in that direction.

ORGANIZATIONAL IDENTITY

An organization must possess a clearly defined identity. Any change in sense of self, be it for an individual or an organization, will have an inevitable, far-reaching trickle-down effect on their beliefs, their skills and on their behaviour generally. That is why it is so important whenever a takeover or merger occurs, that the new organization has a clearly defined identity, different from the old. The identity of an organization gives people a sense of belonging. The larger the organization, the more tenuous this can become. We tend to look to a smaller, personal group to build our sense of identity, which is why small teams can work so well together. Inside some large organizations, people may have a greater loyalty to their department than to the organization, and pursue departmental advantage at the expense of the whole organization. The larger the organization, the more likely this becomes.

As organizations become more horizontal and more networked, with more tasks being subcontracted, there is a danger that the organization's identity is frittered away to subcontractors. You must decide which parts to hand over and which parts to keep. A skill that may seem small and unimportant may be representative of the company's identity. For example, BMW has moved strongly towards collaborative manufacturing. Up to three-quarters of the total production costs come from outsourced parts. BMW prides itself on collaboration with, and learning from, its suppliers without becoming overtly dependent on them, or vulnerable to them. This strategic learning is arguably part of their identity. However, when there was an argument between the purchasing and engineering departments on whether to outsource cylinder heads, they decided to keep production in house, because they did not want to pass this crucial technology to a supplier.

You may find clues to organizational identity in statements by the CEO that begin: 'We are . . .' or, 'This company is . . .'. You can also find them in the company logo and advertisements. A logo is an icon for how the company wants to be seen and organizations are willing to spend large amounts of money on them.

A COSTLY CHANGE OF IDENTITY

BT was once called British Telecom. Do you remember Buzby, used extensively in advertisements for British Telecom? BT decided that they did not want to be identified with an intellectually challenged fluffy bird balancing on a telephone wire, and spent hundreds of thousands of pounds designing and implementing a new logo.

As with individuals, organizational behaviour must be separated from organizational identity. Tim is senior manager of a high technology equipment manufacturer. He told us that his firm was having a difficult time with one of its French distributors. The distributor was not active enough and the company was concerned that it was losing sales. They wanted behavioural level changes. The distributor, however, was completely unresponsive to feedback, so the company acted unilaterally and instituted some minor changes. This led to a very serious breakdown in rapport that seemed bizarre and incomprehensible as a reaction to the changes. It soon became clear that the distributor was offended at the identity level – they felt they would be seen in a bad light. How they looked in the market place was extremely important to them.

Tim went to see them and paced their problem at his meeting. He made it clear that any changes would support their image. He made it clear that his company believed in their integrity and capability and . . . he wanted some behavioural changes. He achieved them, once the problem was paced and behaviour was separated from identity.

KNOWING WHERE TO TAP

Change is possible at any level, the question is: which will have the most leverage – give the greatest result for the smallest effort? A change at the belief level is likely to affect many skills and behaviours, a change in identity even more so. You can work from the top down, or from the bottom up; all the levels relate together systemically.

When you are confronted with a problem, identify the level you are stuck on:

You may need more information from the environment. If so, do nothing until you have gathered the information you need using many different perspectives.

You may have all the information, but not know exactly what to do.

You may know what to do, but not know how to do it.

You may wonder whether you can do it, whether it is worthwhile and if it is in keeping with your beliefs and values, or those of the organization.

And you may want to check if it is in keeping with your sense of self.

You can use this format to help others with problems when they come to you for help.

These levels are very useful in helping to diagnose what is going on organizationally. A few years ago a colleague of ours was working with a multinational computer company at a time of reorganization within the UK division. His brief was to make this process as painless as possible and he was receiving good co-operation from departments within the company with one notable exception. In this particular department people were curiously unavailable and data was not forthcoming. As a seasoned analyst he was perplexed because there was no threat to this department in the reorganization process.

However, it is not enough to be an analyst in such circumstances. In some ways it is also important to be an historian. When he looked into the history of the company he found that seven years previously a large reorganization had resulted in the drastic reduction in size of this particular department and it had not been forgotten. Like individuals, departments and companies and organizations have memories and a biography. They have a history which gives them a sense of self that forms their identity. When they perceive their identity being challenged they will react defensively in order to preserve what they are – all the more so if they fear for their survival.

A manager we know paid much attention to developing his team. He had fought hard to secure a sizeable training budget and encouraged them to take training courses. He believed they were under-performing, partly because of the number of sick days per annum and yet he also believed they were motivated. When he asked us if we had any suggestions we went and talked to some of the people. We asked them a simple question: 'What would be the one change you would most like that would enhance your working?' There was no unanimous agreement. Some people asked that the office layout be redesigned; a couple complained about the amount of highly visible computer cabling in the office. Quite a few told us how they wished they had anti-glare screens for the word processors. What was so striking was that despite the different requests, all of them were about making changes in the working environment. (It is interesting that in recent years the 'office environment' is now used to describe the workplace, rather than plain 'office'. We also now have a 'sick building syndrome'.)

When we told the manager about these concerns, he was genuinely surprised. As a man whose own office window looked straight out onto a brick wall, it was not very surprising that these matters seemed of no great consequence to him. Yet he knew that something was amiss. He decided to humour us. The budget needed for these changes was relatively small and could be accommodated within the present financial year. His preoccupation had been at a capability level, making sure his people had the skills he thought would enhance their performance, and that they valued those training opportunities. However, he had not taken into account that there are other levels which are equally important – and indeed for some people will be even more important.

Making these changes in the environment had two striking effects. The total number of days off sick dropped significantly and also the atmosphere changed. 'People are just more co-operative', he said. Having seen the changes, even though he thought it was crazy, he recognized that changing the environment was clearly important to his people. After that there was no stopping him. Last time we saw him, he asked us what we thought about giving each of his people a personal ionizer. He also told us that he was holding a couple of meetings to ask people what colour schemes they thought would be best for the office when it was redecorated in six months' time.

Many managers are very good at operating at one or two logical levels, however very few are able to function at all five. It is valuable to know your own particular bias. Ask yourself which logical levels do you find it easiest to operate on; at what level do you tend to intervene and at what level do you feel most at ease? Equally important, what level do you feel least at ease with? The behaviour level is the most obvious one to operate on, but do not remain at this level. Managing behaviour is the wrong level. It leads to over-managing and micro-managing. A manager who concentrates on managing behaviour will not be empowering his people. Manage capability and direction rather than behaviour.

Logical levels have a particular place in strategic planning. Whenever you are planning to create change, it is valuable to look at all five levels and know the impact of any proposed change. Such all-round problem solving is rare. Being clear about all levels when creating change means you will have a much fuller idea of the consequences of your plans. Too often people only pay attention to one or two of the levels and so are taken by surprise at what happens when they implement a plan that looks perfectly good on paper.

Suppose you were reorganizing your department or a number of departments. Logical levels will provide you with a framework to ask questions and organize information.

IDENTITY   What needs to be done so the new department has an identity of its own and the people feel a sense of belonging?

BELIEFS   What is important about the new department and how should the principles of running it be identified, articulated, and communicated to the people who work in it, as well as to the clients and potential clients?

CAPABILITIES   The department should be clear what are its special capabilities that differentiate it from other departments. What procedures are required to run this department?

BEHAVIOUR   What ought people to be doing in this new department? What has to happen on a day-to-day basis? What training or retraining is required?

ENVIRONMENT   What office space do we have? Who is working together? What technology do we have?

TAKING THE ORGANIZATIONAL TEMPERATURE

Another application for logical levels is as a means of taking the temperature of your department or organization. One simple device we often use is to ask people what they most like about the organization and what they least like. If you find that the likes are mainly at a level of identity or beliefs and the dislikes are at the level of environment or behaviour, you know there are changes that can be fairly easily made which will be beneficial. Creating changes is invariably easier at an environmental or behavioural level and is going to produce remedial effects. However, if you find the dislikes are at the level of identity and the likes are merely at the level of environment then you have just identified a crucial defect. Such an organization must make a radical reappraisal of how it is perceived by its people, because there is a lack of rapport between their identities and its identity – and that spells trouble potentially.

One final point. Every intervention at any logical level can also affect what goes on at other levels. You can begin anywhere to have an impact. For instance, if you change the environment you may well help people to feel different about themselves and so free untapped potential. A good example is to see how outdoor trainers use the natural environment to give people an experience quite outside their ordinary expectations. Teaching a group of bank clerks to abseil definitely brings out hidden potential, even if it does frighten them initially.

DEVELOPING YOUR SKILLS

1   Consider a current problem you are facing. What level does it seem to stem from? Where will you intervene? Would it be preferable to stay on the same level as the problem, or do you need to address a different level? Test your solution for possible consequences at all five levels.
2   Choose a meeting and identify the logical levels a person is talking from.
3   Watch TV with the sound down and guess on which level the speaker is talking. This way you will get used to picking up visual clues as well. Notice in particular hand gestures. When you see a hand go to the person's midline in the upper chest region, you are almost certainly seeing an identity level statement.
4   Take one logical level per working day and look and listen out for how many examples you come across.

FURTHER READING

Dilts, Robert, *Changing Belief Systems With NLP*, Meta Publications, Cupertino 1990.
O'Connor, Joseph, and McDermott, Ian, *Principles of NLP*, Thorsons 1996.
O'Connor, Joseph, and Seymour, John, *Introducing NLP*, Thorsons 1993.

NOTES

1   Burleson, Clyde, *Interstate Commerce: Regional Styles of Doing Business*, Franklin Watts, New York 1987.

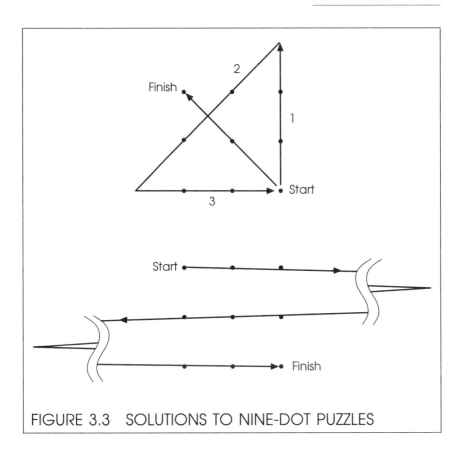

FIGURE 3.3   SOLUTIONS TO NINE-DOT PUZZLES

4
OUTCOMES

❖

Targets. Goals. Objectives. Outcomes. Projects. They may be ways of solving pressing problems, or they may be new initiatives. All these words express the idea of moving from here to there – from a present situation that is unsatisfactory in some way to a desired situation that is better. NLP uses the word 'outcome' rather than 'goal' or 'objective' to describe the results we want, so we shall use it here. The idea of an outcome is also more specific and measurable than a goal or an objective.

It is important to distinguish between outcome and task:

An outcome is what you want.
A task is what you do to achieve it.

There are two important points to consider:

○ Thinking in outcomes sets a direction and a purpose for your actions. Until you know what you want, what you do will be aimless and your results random. Outcome thinking gives you control over the direction in which you travel and is essential in management.

○ Whether you set outcomes or not, you are always obtaining results, only they may not be what you want. How you set up outcomes is important – they need to be realistic, motivating and achievable.

Outcomes have become almost universally known in management largely through the writings of Peter Drucker. Setting outcomes is a way of thinking, not just something to do at certain times. Outcome thinking means being directed towards what you want. It moves you forward.

The opposite to outcome thinking is problem thinking, which concentrates on what is wrong. In an imperfect world there are always problems

57

and in management you do not have to look for them, they find you. There will always be something wrong, and many managers lose themselves in a labyrinth of problems – finding out the history, cost and consequences of problems as well as who to blame. Outcome thinking shifts the question from, 'What's wrong?' to 'What do we want?' Outcome thinking is more than solution thinking. Once you have defined the problem, it takes you towards solutions in a structured way.

THE DIFFERENCE BETWEEN OUTCOME THINKING AND PROBLEM THINKING – THREE-QUARTERS OF A MILLION DOLLARS

Jack Lennard, senior manager in a high technology company based in London, was having trouble with some of his local European distributors. The situation had become so bad that one of their main customers was threatening to return equipment worth half a million dollars, ask for a refund, and reorder from one of their competitors. Not only that, but they were also threatening to sue the distributor for damages. The whole situation looked very bad, and would be a blow for the parent company. Jack was in a meeting with the customer's senior managers who had flown in from Europe. There were certainly enough problems to consider here. The customers were angry. Although they liked doing business with the parent company, the local distributor was a big stumbling block.

Jack paced the customer at the crucial meeting. Yes, he agreed it was a bad situation. Yes, the distributor had made mistakes. Yes, they were quite right to be angry and, yes, we understand why you are threatening to sue. The customers were somewhat taken aback, expecting a contentious meeting. Having paced and gained rapport he then asked the sixty-four thousand dollar question or, in this case, the half-million dollar question: what would it be like if we could find a good solution for you here? This question, a very simple one, moves the emphasis from problem to outcome. However, asked without initial pacing and rapport it is likely to produce the answer, 'See you in court!' It was only possible after first acknowledging and pacing the customer's experience and frustrations.

After a moment's silence, some constructive discussions began. The customer vetoed an initial proposal for settlement as too expensive. Jack asked another question: 'What if we could work out a way that you could afford it?' Together they explored different solutions. The outcome was that instead of returning half a million dollars' worth of equipment, the customer returned only fifty thousand dollars' worth, and placed a further new order of a quarter of a million dollars. They are now a reference site for his company and actively promoting it in the market.

Four elements led to this success:

○   Pacing and leading.
○   Outcome thinking rather than problem thinking.
○   The 'As if' frame. This is the adult version of 'Let's pretend', and allows you to explore the future with questions like, 'What would happen if . . .' or, 'Suppose this happened . . .' It is doing in your mind what computers do when they run simulations of possible future events, and is indispensable to future planning. It helps to create a future you prefer, rather than being bounded in a present you wish to escape from. Also, because it is in the form of 'What if', no one feels pressured to accept any proposal, and it leads to a constructive search.
○   The conditional close. '*If* such and such were to happen, *then* would you . . . ?' It begins to take the 'As if' frame a little further.

TASK AND PROCESS

Good management is a balance between task, what needs to be done – and process, how it is done. Managers face problems in both areas; the task problems are usually more straightforward and more obvious. It is easy to lose your sense of long-term direction in the everyday race to perform the tasks. Yet tasks that are not outcome-focused are likely to be insufficiently considered and poorly planned, and so are also likely to be poorly executed. They may well take longer to execute, thus creating the very problem that led to the task being hurried in the first place – shortage of time. (There is no time to think this out fully – just do it!)

Tasks take you towards your outcomes. For the tasks to be well co-ordinated, complete and fully effective, you need to think in a structured way. This does not mean management by objectives, but it certainly means management with objectives.

Outcome thinking embraces three elements:

Your present situation – where you are now.
Your desired situation – where you want to be.
Your resources – how you are going to move from one to the other.

We have talked to many managers and consultants about management issues. Lack of structured outcome thinking came consistently in their top three management problems. We will consider the process of thinking through management outcomes in detail, both from an individual and organizational point of view. This structure needs to come before the tasks.

LOOKING TWO WAYS AT ONCE

We will look at outcomes on three levels.

First, individual outcomes. Management examples are appraisals, eliciting customer requirements and analysing your own performance. You can use the same process in your personal life as well.

Second, organizational outcomes. These are decided at the higher board levels, and comprise mission statements, corporate strategies and high-level projects. They are necessarily couched in very general terms and have to be translated into smaller outcomes and real tasks at every level of the organization. Setting organizational targets and chunking them into specific tasks that need to be accomplished is a key managerial skill.

Third, the relationship between the organizational and the individual outcomes. How do the sum of the parts add up to the whole? Think of an organization like a river flowing with many different eddies and swirling currents. The force and direction of the river comes from upstream, but the currents can strengthen its direction or divert it. Underwater rocks may break up the current and the stream will lose its force. Rivers never flow completely smoothly with everything aligned – neither do organizations. The more aligned they are, however, the faster and more powerful the flow.

At each level of the organization, the manager must ask two crucial questions:

> How do my outcomes relate and support the higher level outcomes?
> How do the outcomes of my people at the lower levels support or hinder my outcomes?

A manager has to be like the Roman god Janus – able to look in both directions at once. Janus gives his name to the month of January which simultaneously looks to the old year and opens the new.

SETTING OUTCOMES

Stating a problem properly is the key to solving it. There are certain key questions that have to be asked when formulating outcomes. When goals are not thought through clearly, they are impossible to track, maintain and achieve. Project management can become a nightmare without outcome thinking. Many appraisal systems are disappointing, because although they are well structured to track outcomes, the actual outcomes that they track are poorly structured. The individuals concerned do not think through their projects in a clear, structured way.

There are many management acronyms for goal setting – ASMART (Agreed, Specific, Measured, Achievable, Results-oriented and Timed) is one example. NLP goes into more detail, particularly about how outcomes are chunked into tasks at different levels of management.

The value of the following checklist is to bring together in a systematic way all the key questions. As you work through them, you are building your outcome and making it real. Our thoughts guide our actions – sloppy thinking leads to sloppy actions. These questions test your plans and find the defects before the real world does so in a less forgiving way.

POSITIVE – WHAT DO YOU WANT?

Outcomes are expressed in the positive. This has nothing to do with 'positive thinking – everything is OK'. Positive here means directed towards something you want rather than away from something you want to avoid. Ask 'What do I want?' not 'What do I not want?'

Personal goals such as 'I want to give up smoking' and 'I want to lose weight' are not outcomes because they are both expressed in the negative (so it is no surprise that they are both difficult to achieve). Setting negative outcomes is like going shopping with a list of things you do not want to buy – very time consuming and frustrating. Any outcome with words like 'less', 'stop', 'give up', or reduce' is likely to be negative.

There is another problem about negative outcomes. Suppose we say, 'Don't think about your office.' You have to think about the office in order to understand the instruction. You have to do what you are told not to do in order to understand it in the first place! When people think about losing weight and giving up smoking, they are concentrating on the smoking or the fat, rather than the change they seek. Make your outcomes those of aspiration, not desperation.

It is no different in management. Reducing waste, cutting fixed costs, and losing fewer key staff are all negative outcomes. We were consulting for one executive who said he wanted to reduce the total company debt. This was extremely important, the company was facing closure. When we asked him what he actually wanted, he replied that he wanted to improve the company cash flow because if he could do that, it would improve the balance sheet, so assets would exceed liabilities and the company would be more creditworthy. There are many possibilities for improving cash flow and he thought of several immediately. He was then able to turn these into outcomes that ultimately kept the company in business. The two key measures turned out to be increasing the total number of orders and making the multinational management team work well together.

Many management decisions are made to avoid adverse consequences. Fear is a powerful influence, and some risks are unacceptable. Safety is the positive outcome of fear. Instead of being driven reactively to avoid risk for fear of the consequences, organizations can take positive steps to ensure their own safety. Fear paralyses. Safety is a springboard from which to act. It is interesting that Deming's famous formulation 'Driving fear out of the organization' is itself a negative outcome.

How do you turn a negative into a positive outcome?

Ask two simple questions:

> 'What do I want instead?'
> 'What will this do for me?'

For example, one sales manager stated his outcome to us as, 'I want to reduce the number of complaints in the customer service division.'

'What will this do for you?' 'I'll know that we have more satisfied customers.' 'So what do you want?' 'More satisfied customers.'

This was an outcome we could work with. It was the difference between trying to eradicate the symptom and discovering the cause. He knew that in achieving it he would automatically reduce the number of complaints.

EVIDENCE – HOW WILL YOU KNOW YOU HAVE SUCCEEDED?

There must be some way of measuring success; a race is endless if there is no finishing line. You need feedback. The most immediate and compelling feedback channels are your senses. What will you see, hear and feel when you have achieved your outcome? You may also consider the question 'How will others know when I have achieved this?' What will they see, hear and feel? Will it appear differently to them?

There are two important principles of feedback:

O   Obtain ongoing feedback as soon as you can, so that you can track the progress towards your outcome. Feedback that comes too late is not helpful.

O   Ask the questions that will give you the feedback you desire. This may mean, for example, paying careful attention to the design of customer feedback forms.

An everyday example is the oil pressure light in your car. You want it to come on as soon as the oil pressure drops too low, not the next day when the engine has been damaged. And you want the sensor to be reliable, and not tell you oil pressure is too low when in fact it is normal.

Last year Ian was working with a senior manager who wanted his production team and his admin people to work well together. At that time, they hardly met at all, let alone worked well together. The office and plant were built round a courtyard. On one side was production, on the other, about one hundred yards away, was administration. When Ian asked the manager what he would see if he achieved his outcome of bringing the management team together, he talked of people physically walking across the courtyard and consulting each other. Asked what he would hear, he said the two groups talking and making decisions together. Asked what he would feel, he said that a weight would be lifted from his shoulders. Even as he said this, his shoulders relaxed and he sat a little taller in his seat. If this happened it would also demonstrate that teamwork was not dependent on his invoking the management hierarchy. He need not feel so responsible for them. Previously, when he thought about it all, what came into his mind was people expecting him to tell them what to do. In his new pictures he saw them talking together and making decisions independently. He could at last visualize a resolution.

Making computer models of projects to minimize the risk of going over budget uses the same principle – visualizing a solution. For example, VSEL at Barrow-in-Furness developed an Integrated Modelling Environment (IME) to describe the required system in complete pictures. As Stuart Colvin, a design manager at VSEL's systems division said, 'We realized that to start by choosing the nuts and bolts, and then trying to fit them together is a crazy methodology because the individual components are rarely designed to work as an integrated whole. It makes much more sense to start out with a clear definition of the system you are trying to build, and only then look for the components.'[1]

Virtual reality systems use the same principles. Computers build a model that people can interact with – see and hear how it will be through a virtual reality headset that presents sounds and pictures. Architects can make a model of a building and give clients the experience of walking through it in virtual reality. The building exists only in the imagination of the architect and the circuits of the computer, yet the experience is realistic.

We have the ultimate computer between our ears. We can not only make pictures, but add sounds and feelings, make it moving or still, large or small. No virtual reality system has enough memory to make all the possible changes we can make mentally in an instant . Once you have a picture of how you want it to be, then it is much easier to design feedback systems to tell you how you are progressing, because you know what you are looking for.

SPECIFIC – WHERE, WHEN AND WITH WHOM?

Where do you want the outcome? Which places specifically? There may be places and situations where you do not want the outcome. You may want to increase productivity, but only in certain departments. You may want to buy a particular building, but not if interest rates rise beyond a certain point.

When do you want it? You may need to meet a deadline. Sometimes you may not want the outcome before a specific date either, because other elements would not be in place to take advantage of it. One director told us how he burnt his fingers by not considering this. He had decided that he wanted to increase sales, but in going all out to do so, he succeeded too quickly and created many frustrated customers who could not take delivery because of insufficient stock. Management is rather like cooking, where timing is everything. Act too soon and your plans are half baked, act too late and they're burnt.

Large organizational projects are necessarily clothed in fluffy language. They need to be translated into specifics where people can take action. Ian was asked to resolve an interdepartmental dispute in a medium-sized manufacturing company. The 'bare facts' were that department A wanted department B to increase productivity. The head of department B thought this was absurd, because his department had no means of coping with an increased throughput. On closer inspection it turned out that A did not actually want to increase the total throughput, instead it was trying to overcome a bottleneck in its own production process by requiring B to produce each of the components faster. The words 'increased productivity' had a different meaning for each party. The head of department A did not want more components, but the same number of components faster. When this was clear to the head of the other department, and he knew exactly what had to be done, the problem disappeared.

WHAT ARE YOUR RESOURCES?

Gather your resources. They will fall into five categories:

○ What objects do you have? Examples would be office equipment, buildings, and computer equipment.
○ What people can help you? There are the people you manage, higher level managers, consultants, customers, suppliers, other business contacts and friends.
○ What role models are available? Do you know anyone who has completed a similar project successfully? It does not have to be the

same scale, or even in the same business. Who can you talk to? There may be books you can read, for example Sir John Harvey-Jones, Richard Branson and Ricardo Semler have all written first-hand accounts of dealing with management problems.

O   What personal qualities do you possess? Don't be modest. Do you have and will you need persistence, flexibility, capacity for hard work, ability to see many different perspectives? What qualities must you develop to bring this project to a successful conclusion? (Ability to function on two hours' sleep a night . . . ?) Think of your personal skills and capabilities.

O   Lastly, the proverbial bottom line – what is your budget? What money do you have for the task? Is it enough?

CAN YOU START AND MAINTAIN THIS OUTCOME?

Suppose your aim is to increase sales. If you rely passively upon the market to do this for you, you are not starting or maintaining any new activity. If you leave it to your sales force to sell more, your input is minimal. While the sales team may ultimately achieve the increase, it is for you to facilitate that in whatever way you can.

How much is under your direct control? Think exactly what you can do and what others have to do to achieve this outcome. If you delegate, how and to whom? How can you motivate them to *want* to do it rather than feeling they *have* to do it? How can you persuade and influence others to help you?

WHAT ARE THE WIDER CONSEQUENCES?

You drop a stone in a pool. How far do you track the ripples? There is always collateral damage (and benefit) if you follow the ripples far enough. You always achieve more than you bargained for. Sometimes these effects are trivial, other times your solution becomes a new problem waiting for another solution. The legendary King Midas thought the golden touch was a great idea. He did not foresee the dreadful consequences of *everything* he touched turning to gold.

Here are some wider, systemic questions to consider:

O   What time and effort will this outcome require? Everything has an opportunity cost. Time and effort spent on one thing leaves others neglected.

O   Who else is affected and how will they feel? Look at different perspectives: your boss, your customers, your suppliers and the people you manage. What you learn may transform your outcome, or suggest a better way to achieve it.

○   What will you have to give up when you achieve this outcome? There are aspects of the present situation that you will want to keep. Make sure you do.
○   What else could happen when I achieve what I want?
○   What will I lose if I achieve what I want? And is that acceptable?

These are interesting questions. They will challenge and smoke out restricting beliefs in individuals and departments. Non co-operation and resistance to change are nearly always driven by beliefs about what would happen if . . . Other perspectives, if ignored, may sabotage your efforts.

As you tease out the by-products of the status quo, you will also discover the hidden agendas which have been preventing change. We remember one managing director whose company was in dire financial straits and yet we had the impression that it did not bother him too much. There was much huffing and puffing, but the house had been standing for two years and he had kept the wolf from the door. He seemed to enjoy being the tough man and fed off the anxiety of the people in the company. Eventually they sacked him, and when he was leaving he called the workforce together and gave them a rather rambling lecture.

'Do you know why I joined the parachute regiment when I was young?' he asked them. Of course nobody did, although there were some muttered and unrepeatable guesses.

'I joined because I was afraid of heights.' For those who had ears to hear, that was a revelation. Here was a man who had learnt to defeat his fear by doing the thing that most triggered it.

Once he was deposed, the company's fortunes revived remarkably. Now there was no one at the helm who needed to be fighting for survival in order to rise to a challenge. The challenge now was to build the company and make it successful.

IS THIS OUTCOME IN KEEPING WITH WHO YOU ARE?

You can apply this identity question at both the individual and organizational level.

First, the individual level. Suppose you have an outcome to work on a project team that is being formed. Now you ask this question. Being involved with this project would mean spending a great deal of time away from home travelling. It would mean dropping some other projects you are engaged in and would take you at a tangent to your main career path. Although you would like to be involved, on balance it does not suit you. You might ask, 'What does working on this project team accomplish for me?' If the answer is to gain valuable experience, then there may be other projects; or training and consulting might be preferable – for you.

The same is true at the organizational level. Each company has a certain culture and a set of core values that define its identity. Company outcomes need to be congruent – in keeping with this corporate self. Many companies fail by diversifying into areas where they are ignorant, and which do not fit their identity. The expansion of Sock Shop into America was a disaster and precipitated many problems. As ever, the three most important things about real estate are – location, location and location. Sock Shop bought shops in areas where even the most brilliant management would have been hard pressed to trade a profit.

Many a company has a strong identity that is characteristic of its founder, and this can work to its advantage. Richard Branson of Virgin started an airline – a pursuit somewhat removed from his original music business, but he and Virgin are identified with entrepreneurship and innovation, so the move worked well. He also researched his target market thoroughly before acting.

CHINESE BOXES – HOW DO OUTCOMES FIT TOGETHER?

Have you seen a series of Chinese boxes? Each one is smaller than the one it fits into. How does your outcome fit in with your higher level plans? When you are frustrated in a big outcome, identify what prevents you from continuing, and set a smaller outcome to clear the hurdle.

When you feel bogged down with minutiae, ask yourself what does this achieve for you, and connect the details to the larger, more motivating outcome of which it forms part.

This is a very important aspect of outcomes in an organization. How do the projects fit into the corporate strategy? Are the tasks and projects aligned with the higher level purposes of the organization?

Chapter 5 will deal with this in detail.

ACTION PLAN

Once you have put your plan through these questions, you can act yourself, and delegate to others. When delegating, give your people the wider picture, so they can connect their tasks with the larger project. Make sure they know how to think outcomes through for themselves, so the process is iterated all the way down. This will ensure that their tasks are thought through and aligned with yours. When outcomes are aligned up and down the organization, the cross currents are reinforcing the flow in the direction you want.

You must track the following information in any project that you manage:

O   Who is responsible? Who is the leader of this project? On whose desk does the buck come to rest?
O   Who is involved? What tasks are they carrying out?
O   What roles will people play?
O   Who needs to be kept informed?

COMPUTER-ASSISTED OUTCOME SETTING

Many companies are starting to use computer software to form and keep track of outcomes. The advantages are that the software can ask the questions in a structured way, and the results can be stored in whatever way the user selects, and used in project meetings as a shared resource. Sometimes it is difficult to keep team discussion focused. The computer solves this problem by becoming a centre for a team to work together on the outcome they want. We have designed software that explicitly goes through this process[2] so outcomes can be sorted and clarified. (See 'Training and resources', p. 193, for details of outcome software.)

REQUIREMENTS ELICITATION

These outcome questions are invaluable for finding out exactly what your customers want, whether they are internal or external to your organization. Few organizations would disagree with the idea of meeting the customers' need, yet many are not very good at discovering exactly what these needs are. They guess, and then meet their guesswork. They may be lucky. They may not. Needs are not always well defined, and customers are not always lucid about them; but they will certainly blame you if you don't give them what they want. It is the company's responsibility to elicit from the customer.

Use the outcome questions not only to clarify what the customer wants, so that you can supply it first time, but also when you are the customer. One company we know spent a large amount of money installing a new data storage system on the advice of its technical staff. The technical staff recommended the most up-to-date system. What was important to them was how easy the system was to operate. Unfortunately, being easy to operate was no advantage when it was discovered somewhat belatedly that the system was not very good at doing what the management needed it to do. It happens every day – outcomes have not been dovetailed. In management this can be very costly. Computer systems are like clothes. They can be new, fashionable and fun to wear, but they also need to fit.

TWO PER CENT CORRECT

In 1979 US government accounting office figures for commissioned software showed *47 per cent* of the software ordered was delivered but *never used*. An enormous waste of money.

Twenty-nine per cent was paid for but never delivered.

Nineteen per cent was used but only after extensively reworking the software.

Three per cent was used after minor changes.

Two per cent was used as delivered. This was actually a COBOL pre-processor. The requirements were simple, the problem was understood and the personnel involved all had a computing background.

We wonder how much these figures have improved over the years.

There are many reasons why requirements elicitation can fail and most of them relate to unanswered outcomes questions. Firstly, a management problem is often framed as a negative: something is going wrong and needs to be put right. It is impossible to develop a solution unless the problem is turned into a positive outcome.

You must also find out the kind of problem.

O   Is it a clearly defined problem in a clearly defined context? For example, designing a software package to track departmental budgets. The figures and the processes are already in use; they need bringing together in the most effective way. There may be existing models that can be used to save design time.

O   Is it a clearly defined problem in an unknown context? For example, when companies move into new business areas, they need information about the new domain.

O   Are both the scope and the problem undefined? Here you need multiple perspectives and an analysis of logical levels to define the space of the problem before asking the outcome questions.

Remember rapport. The quality of answers to the questions will depend on it. Grilling the customer like the Spanish Inquisition, even with the best intention, may be counterproductive.

ORGANIZATIONAL PURPOSE – WHAT DO WE WANT?

The original companies were formed when a group of people came together to achieve an outcome greater than any individual could attain alone. Their purpose was to make some money for investors. Many increased the public good, either as a by-product of pursuing their own long-term interests, or from altruism. Organizations have many purposes at the highest level. The main ones are:

○   To make a profit.
○   To secure the employment, security, fame and fortune of those people who run the company.
○   To share risk.

Profit is sometimes allowed to overshadow other purposes, to the extent that it is regarded as the only purpose of being in business. What is the purpose of your organization? In many management courses, the 1960s answer lingers on: 'To maximize the medium-term earning per share'. This is questionable under the following considerations:

To make as big as *possible?*
What are the ethical restraints?
What are the structural constraints?
What are the wider consequences to the people and to the environment?
How long is the medium-term – three months, six months, two weeks?
Does pursuing profit in the medium-term lead to long-term disaster?

One organizational purpose that is often not sufficiently thought through is survival. How big does a risk have to be before it is unacceptable? In any complex system if you maximize one variable you *inevitably* weaken other areas. A better formulation might be to 'optimize the medium-term earning per share'.

What are the values implications if profitability for shareholders is taken as the primary purpose of an organization? When managers' rewards are linked to the share price, they become allied with the shareholders rather than the workers. This sets them apart. When managers are shareholders, workers and other stakeholders tend to be counted as costs, and costs are something to be reduced. This questions the issue of people being seen as the company's greatest resource. Are people costs or assets on the company balance sheet?

Shareholders may be able to make more profit by withdrawing money from the business than by allowing it to invest in itself. Since 1975 British companies have retained an average of 45 per cent of their profits for reinvestment. This compares with 54 per cent for American firms, 63 per cent for Japanese firms, and 67 per cent for German firms. If profitability is the main organizational purpose, then the natural consequence of this way of thinking would seem to be for shareholders to take their money out of British firms and invest it abroad in companies that act as if they believe more in their own long-term future.

All companies need to make money; without a revenue stream, there is no organization. There are millions of companies round the world all wanting to make money. What makes your organization different? Organizational values provide one answer. They will structure *how* you make money. When purpose is allied to values, money ceases to be the prime directive. It is a means to an end, a by-product rather than an end product. It can be seen as evidence that the organization is doing things right. When an organization is serving the customer it will both keep business and acquire repeat business. It will be financially successful, therefore making money shows it is serving the customer well.

Values are what get people out of bed in the morning. How inspiring is the aim to 'maximize medium-term earnings per share'? Is it likely to make hearts beat faster?

The secret of successful managing is to translate the organizational purpose into successful tasks and projects that give people what they want: self-respect, recognition, the sense of belonging and mastery. First we will consider the Chinese boxes problem – how can organizational purpose be successfully chunked down to manageable projects? Then we will look to the level of organizational values that combine with purpose to create vision, and how they support individual values.

OUTCOME SUMMARY

1   POSITIVE – WHAT DO I WANT?

Outcomes should be expressed in the positive. That is, moving towards a desired goal and not away from something undesirable.

Questions:

What would this outcome do for me if I achieved it?
What do I want instead?

2   EVIDENCE – HOW WILL I KNOW I HAVE SUCCEEDED?

Decide in advance what is the evidence that will let you know you have achieved the outcome.

The evidence will be what you will see, hear and feel when you have achieved your outcome.

Questions:

> How will I know that I have achieved my outcome?
>
> What will I be seeing, hearing and feeling when I have achieved it?
>
> What will others be seeing, hearing and feeling when I have achieved it?

3   SPECIFIC – WHERE, WHEN AND WITH WHOM?

Questions:

> Where do I want this outcome?
>
> When do I want this outcome?
>
> With whom do I want this outcome?
>
> Are there times, places and people where I do not want it?

4   WHAT ARE MY RESOURCES?

Questions:

> What objects do I have as resources?
>
> What personal qualities?
>
> Which people could help?
>
> What role models do I have?
>
> What is the budget?

5   CAN I START AND MAINTAIN THIS OUTCOME?

Questions:

> What can I do directly to achieve my outcome?
>
> What is under and what is outside my control?
>
> What can I do to persuade and influence others to help me?

6   WHAT ARE THE WIDER CONSEQUENCES?

Questions:

> What time and effort are required to achieve this outcome?
>
> What money investment does this goal need?
>
> Who else is affected and how will they feel about this?
>
> What will I have to give up when I achieve this outcome?
>
> What is good about my present circumstances?
>
> How can I keep what is positive about the present situation?

7   IS THIS OUTCOME IN KEEPING WITH WHO I AM?

Questions:

> Is the outcome aligned with my identity?
> Do I feel congruent about this outcome?
> Is this the way we do things?

8   HOW DOES THIS OUTCOME FIT IN WITH OTHER OUTCOMES?

Questions:

> What larger outcome is this part of?
> What smaller outcomes need to be achieved to overcome obstacles?

9   WHAT IS THE ACTION PLAN?

Questions:

> Who is responsible?
> Who is involved?
> What roles will people play?
> Who needs to be kept informed?

DEVELOPING YOUR SKILLS

1   Use the outcome questions to structure your projects.
2   Use the outcome questions in teams to guide you to the result you all want.
3   Use the outcome questions with customers at every level to find out what they want. Remember to obtain rapport first.
4   Use the outcome process for self-appraisal every six months.

FURTHER READING

Drucker, Peter, *The Effective Executive*, Heinemann 1967.
Harvey-Jones, Sir John, *Making It Happen*, HarperCollins 1994.

NOTES

1   'VSEL', *Sunday Times*, 13 May 1990.
2   Goal Wizard Outcome Software, ITS Software 1994.

5

FROM PURPOSE TO PRACTICE

This chapter is about two principles:

1   How do you translate from the high-level organizational purpose to concrete projects – what does it mean in practice?
2   Understanding the level of detail at which you are working.

The organizational purpose is the big picture. To implement it we need a strategy – how the purpose will be accomplished. Together they make a mission statement:

Purpose + Strategy = Mission

The mission cascades down the organization into multi-level tasks and projects. Working at the level of mission will affect all the organization. The higher the level you are working at, the more of the organization is involved. The mission sets the direction for the whole organization. It is the largest of the Chinese boxes. Different projects, research and development will be initiated to support the mission

Some problems are not solvable unless you work at this high level; others can be solved at a lower level. Imagine a power station. The purpose is rather like an electrical generator – it produces power. The strategy is the layout of pipes and cables that brings the power to all the parts of the building. Each part of the organization can use the power to carry out projects, tasks and maintenance. To continue the analogy, if you have a fuse that keeps blowing, it is not very useful to tamper with the generator, although you might theoretically solve the problem by reducing the power output. If there is a power cut, it is no good installing more light sockets.

CORE BUSINESS OBJECTIVES

Here is a good example of the highest chunk level taken from the 1994 annual report and accounts of the Virtuality group plc – a company that deals in the technology of virtual reality. Joseph is a shareholder and received the report when we were writing this chapter.

The report states that Virtuality's core business objectives are to:

O   generate financial gains for shareholders by creating a high margin, £100 million plus turnover business by the end of the decade

O   build Virtuality as an international brand and to participate in the development of global VR standards

O   maximize the efficiency of the group by achieving high revenues per employee.

The group strategy to achieve these objectives is:

O   to remain the world's leading VR entertainment company by continually refining its technologies and improving price performance ratios

O   to create a compatible range of VR products which will compete for a significant share in evolving VR markets

O   to license its proprietary VR technologies to strategic partners in a wide variety of industries

O   to recruit highly talented individuals and provide them with an environment which encourages innovation and responsibility.

CHINESE BOXES AND CHINESE WHISPERS

Managers need to be able to translate the high-level projects and purpose into specific tasks, and to manage these tasks so they add up to the whole. This is called *chunking down*, taking a complex task and decomposing it into its components. Every project must be chunked down – like Chinese boxes, the complete project is made up of smaller projects within it.

Purpose, strategies, mission statements and project plans are expressed in words. The higher the level, the more general the words. The mission statement will be very general and necessarily so. The words are not the tasks, and words on their own can be misleading. You must be clear in your own mind what has to be done, and must be able to tell others clearly what they should do. Words are the currency of management. We read or hear them, make sense of them and pass on that sense to others by writing or speaking. However, two things can go wrong:

O   We may misunderstand the original words and take action on *our* meaning and not the intended one.

O   Others may misunderstand what we tell them and take action on *their* meaning, not what we intended.

The result can be like a game of Chinese whispers, where a project can be totally misunderstood by the time it reaches the end of the line and the sum of the parts is nothing like the original idea.

Miscommunications happen all the time, because words do not have fixed meanings. They mean what we think they mean. One person interprets the meaning of key words and acts on it, rather than asking the speaker what they mean. The consequences in management can be painfully expensive. We need to ask questions to find out what the other person's statement means, whether it is a memo, a project plan, or the mission statement of the company. We need to be clear in our own minds, and have the communication skills to clarify for others exactly what has to be done.

One reason why projects fail is that managers are not sufficiently rigorous in asking exact questions designed to elicit information. The higher the level of the plan, the more abstract the language becomes. The words carry many possible interpretations. An important first step to project management is clarity of language.

KEY QUESTIONS

Words do not automatically convey their intended meaning. The listeners act on the meaning they themselves make, which is not necessarily the one intended, so you need a set of questions to clarify ambiguities. NLP has such a communication tool. It is called the Meta Model.

The Meta Model was developed by Richard Bandler and John Grinder and was first published in 1975 in their book, *The Structure of Magic*. The Meta Model is a series of questions that clarify language. When we express an idea in language there are three possible outcomes:

> We *generalize* from a particular example as if it represents all possibilities.
> We *delete* or ignore facts.
> We *distort* the situation by giving descriptive words a meaning they do not support.

These processes are not bad in themselves. Distortion for example, is a source of creativity, seeing new meanings in familiar facts. We learn by generalizing from examples, and must be selective about what we notice and discuss. When we give examples in this book, we must inevitably leave out information, or the book would be as long as the *Encyclopaedia Britannica*. We give examples to make a wider point – we invite you to generalize from them.

The Meta Model is a series of questions designed to unravel language to avoid misunderstandings. It clarifies communication for both speaker and listener, by prompting the speaker to fill in important missing information, reshape the language if it is misleading, and connect generalities with specific examples. Obtaining the right answer depends on asking the right question.

WHO EXACTLY?

Suppose a manager says to you: 'They need this project completed by next month. See the people concerned and find out what has to be done.' 'No--

one is mentioned specifically in the example. Who are the people concerned? The speaker is assuming you know, yet his idea may be different from yours. So be on the look out for words like 'people', 'personnel', or the all-embracing 'they'. Also when the passive tense is used the person it refers to is deleted from the sentence. For example, 'The report was completed' or 'the order was mislaid' deletes the person or people who carried out the action. The passive tense can be used to avoid responsibility; it describes an action without the person who carried it out.

The Meta Model question 'Who exactly?' helps to specify on the logical level of identity. Managing processes means managing the people who carry them out.

WHAT EXACTLY?

Every mission statement is an outcome statement that is not well specified. This is as it should be when working at that level. For example, the Virtuality statement does not specify which technologies it is going to refine, or exactly which price performance ratios it is going to improve.

Another example: 'We must take steps to ensure that this situation never happens again'. A previous discussion may have clarified what this means, but it might still be worth asking. What steps? And which situation? Or another example: 'The computing equipment needs to be upgraded'. Which equipment exactly?

Certain key words may be ambiguous, and have different meanings for different people, which can have wide ranging consequences. There is a good example in *The Fifth Discipline Fieldbook*.[1] An American chemical company was holding a meeting of its worldwide distribution network. The purpose of the meeting was to draft a mission statement. The phrase 'an international distributor' appeared in the first paragraph. A German executive wanted to change the word 'international' to 'global'. The American contingent said the two words meant the same thing, so why bother? The German found it hard to put the difference into words, so he moved to the flipchart. He drew a picture of a wheel with America as the hub and the other nations as the spokes. 'That is international,' he said. 'You are at the centre, you decide.' He then drew what 'global' meant: a wheel with the mission at the hub and America as a spoke like all the other countries. A two-hour debate followed. At the end, the American group realized that there was a difference. Indeed the two words were distinct because they each hid a different way of thinking. They realized they had been dominating the discussions and this had led to difficulties in reaching markets in other countries and attracting good managers outside America.

HOW EXACTLY?

This is the key management question: How do you implement the company strategy? A strategy gives direction, and has to be broken down into a sequence of steps, like a journey. The mission statement gives a map.

Here are some examples. 'Customer satisfaction must be increased', 'Operating costs must come down', 'Personnel need to learn how to operate the accounts'. How exactly are these tasks to be done? This is a capability question. No strategy statement is going to give the details of exactly how it will be accomplished.

MISSION NEW YORK!

Imagine a journey from London to New York. Top management sets the strategy – air travel. There are now a whole sequence of middle management steps to consider, like which flight, what day, which airline. Finally, on a smaller chunk level, booking the flights, taking a taxi to the airport, obtaining local currency etc. Neither top nor middle management is going to issue instructions on how to book the taxi; they attend to their own chunk levels. To translate this into logical levels, each manager must be clear about what is to be done and their own behaviour in the project. They do not try to manage the behaviour of their people or partners.

ONGOING SITUATIONS?

There is one pattern that combines all three of the preceding ones. Look at some of the words in the Virtuality statement – development, standards, efficiency, technologies, innovation, responsibility. These words are examples of what linguists call nominalizations, that is, verbs that have been turned into nouns. Management is another example. Large-scale projects and strategies will necessarily contain nominalizations, because they are vague enough to carry many meanings within them.

Nominalizations are the language patterns of higher management. They are vague on all three of the previous counts – who exactly, what exactly and how exactly. The translation down the organization of mission statements and strategy is largely a process of increasingly denominalizing the concepts.

Nominalizations are very common in business and bureaucracies. We saw a business letter recently that contained the following sentence: 'It has become necessary to review our business relationship. The ongoing situation means that new parameters have become operational.' Nominalizations are very abstract, and very vague, which explains why they are so popular with politicians. Every time a process – a verb – is turned into a thing – a noun – a new nominalization is born. Losing money is a process. If however, the company reports a 'downturn in profits' it has made a thing out of the process. That thing is rather vague and undefined and will have different meanings to different people. When you think about it visually, losing money is like a movie. There is movement, something is happening. A downturn in profits is static, it is like a still photograph. Nominalizations take movies and make them into stills and the process is usually deadening.

Because nominalizations are no longer verbs, they have lost the actors. All the previous questions apply: Who exactly is involved? What exactly is involved? And how exactly did it happen? Nominalizations are dangerous because we take these empty words or phrases and supply the missing details from our own ideas. How much of a downturn and over what period of time? How did it happen and who was involved? In giving the phrase substance we may well imagine answers to these questions and then assume that our speculations are right and even imagine that they were there in the original statement. What's more, the speakers themselves may not be clear about what lies behind their statement. Your questions will force them to think back more clearly to their actual experience and clarify it for themselves, as well as for you.

Recognizing nominalizations is very easy; they are verbs with particular suffixes. The most common are -ship, or -ation, or -ment. The word nominalization itself is a nominalization. Any word that makes sense with 'ongoing' in front of it is almost certainly a nominalization. So while we could talk of an ongoing situation, it would sound strange to refer to an ongoing book. Finally you could ask: 'Can I put it in a wheelbarrow?' Try putting productivity in a wheelbarrow. On the other hand, faced with ordinary nouns like car, shoe, computer, or even office party, you could put these in a wheelbarrow, although you might need a rather large one for the party.

The trick with nominalizations is to turn them back into processes. For example, there is no such thing as a management relationship, but a great deal of relating goes on in management. We were once approached by a CEO to help with 'plans to improve company interpersonal communication'. We asked him: 'How specifically can we improve the way people communicate with each other?' Suddenly the issue had become real and he proceeded to give us a list of half a dozen different ways in which this could be achieved. We summarized these and added some of our own. Out of this grew a programme which we successfully implemented. He was surprised how easy it was to provide positive suggestions once he had turned the abstraction into a process where people were doing things.

NOMINALIZATIONS

verb	noun
to understand	understanding
to communicate	communication
to motivate	motivation
to develop	development
to train	training
to be efficient	efficiency
to manage	management
to organize	organization
to appraise	appraisal
to decide	decision

Here are some other nominalizations. What verb would you use for them?

?	technology
?	business
?	project
?	team
?	goal
?	quality

We have discussed nominalizations at length because they are so important and can be so misleading. They have implications far beyond specifying your outcome. The word 'business' itself of course is a nominalization. There are verbs behind the word 'business'. 'Quality' is another interesting nominalization. The verb behind 'quality' must be something like 'assessing', 'measuring' or 'qualifying'. Now we can ask several more questions:

Who is measuring?
What is being measured?
How is it being measured?
What criteria or standards are being applied?
What are the threshold values for the criteria? (A threshold value must be met without exception, otherwise it is a guideline. Guaranteed next day delivery is a threshold.)

These questions are all useful for chunking down – bringing out the specifics in general instructions. Notice that there are no 'why' questions here. 'Why' questions will elicit beliefs and values (or empty justifications) which we will consider later, they do not help in specifying the tasks to be carried out.

BUZZ PHRASE GENERATOR

Take one word from each column and create an impressive management phrase with which to baffle and impress colleagues. Feel free to add the word 'process' after each phrase for extra impact:

relationship	situation	business
organization	company	project
dedication	management	capability
quality	productivity	operation
margin	turnover	development
efficiency	strategy	technology
enhanced	mobility	programming
functional	modular	objective
conflict	environment	consultancy

For example: business strategy objective, functional conflict technology, or productivity margin development.
    We leave this now to your creativity.

Nominalizations are not bad in themselves as long as you do not mistake them for reality, or think you know what someone else means by them. They are necessary at board level, and you must be alert to translate them into action by asking:

> What is the verb behind this?
> Who is doing this?
> What is being done?
> How will they know they have succeeded?

With clear language, we will now examine two ways to put the mission into practice throughout the organization – through teams and appraisals.

TEAMS

This is the age of teams. They are a key part of every enterprise and are increasingly recognized as the main unit for carrying out objectives. You may already be part of a pre-existing team or you may have to create and manage a project-based team. What is a team? A team is a group of people who act together to create a result that none of them could achieve separately, and all share in the achievement. Organizations are beginning to recognize this, although achievements are still measured and rewarded in terms of individuals.

All members of the team learn something, and if that learning is not to be lost, there must be a review and debrief procedure. This knowledge then should be made public so that others can learn from their colleagues' mistakes and successes. Whatever the result, the team may discover an even better way to be used next time.

Learning is knowledge and knowledge is power. In the past it was the managers that had access to scarce resources like knowledge – they knew how things should be done, and told others to do them. Knowledge helps to maintain position. It gives job security in uncertain times. Team development can threaten this. Team building can threaten individuals who feel insecure and still believe that knowledge and results come from the individual, and when the organization also thinks in this way, it compounds the problem. An organization that has compartmentalized learning, and where people keep the learning to themselves, is not fully effective. The most effective manager is a good team player. Organizations will recognize this when teams deliver results that a collection of individuals could not give.

THE PRISONERS' DILEMMA

Trust is the most important team quality. First, trust that the team is an effective way of working: co-operation achieves results. Second, trust between team members is the basis of a good working relationship, team learning and superior results. Management can learn a great deal by examining how teams operate in sports. A great football team is more than the sum of individual talents, and a national side does not necessarily contain all the most outstanding players up and down the country. The players trust and complement each other, work together and all share in the team's victory.

Trust and co-operation are part of enlightened self-interest which is illustrated in an interesting game used in team building, known as the prisoners' dilemma. The simplest form is a card game between two teams. Each team has ten hearts and ten spades, only the suit matters, not the individual card value. Here are the rules:

> Without prior consultation with the other team, each team plays a card face upwards at the same time.
> If both teams play a heart, each team scores three points.

If your team plays a heart and the other plays a spade, you lose six points and they score six points.
If your team plays a spade and they play a heart, you score six points and they lose six points.
If you both play a spade, you both lose three points.

There are ten rounds. The object of the game is for your team to score as many points as possible. It soon becomes apparent that the only way you can maximize your team's score is to trust the other team. It also brings beliefs about co-operation into the open. What do you play first? Signal co-operation with a heart, or play safe with a spade? When each team trusts the other, both score highly. When they do not, both score poorly. The game gives a different view of co-operation and competition. Both teams have to co-operate for both to achieve a high score. When a co-operator plays with a kindred spirit both will quickly make mutually beneficial moves (hearts). When a co-operator and a competitor play, the co-operator is forced to compete in self-defence. Competitors always play a cut-throat game. Competitive behaviour evokes competitive behaviour in retaliation. Co-operative behaviour does not evoke mutual co-operation in the same way. So a person who sees the world full of competitors and selfish opportunists will excite that very behaviour and so confirm their belief.

The prisoners' dilemma highlights these points:

O   Competitive behaviour will evoke similar behaviour.
O   Mutual co-operation achieves the best results.
O   Mistrust and competition within an organization is both self-sustaining and self-defeating. Where there is trust, everybody wins. Where there is no trust, everyone will follow suit in self-defence. Trust is related to rapport. When people in the organization have rapport skills, people will trust each other.

Good teams are a pleasure to work in, and can accomplish great tasks. The members may be spread throughout the world, coming together only in cyberspace, through electronic mail, or telephone video conferencing. They may be around the same table. The team may be made up of company workers, managers, technical experts, customers, suppliers, and outside consultants.

A team comes together for a purpose. They must be outcome-focused. Beyond that, they must care about the project – it must be important to them. The team needs a shared vision, without which they will be only a collection of individuals and miss the synergy and possibility of greater results that come from team working.

THE FIRE PROJECT

One example of managing change that Joseph had the opportunity of observing closely concerned a particularly important and successful software project in a large communications company. One part of the business had decided that to be more responsive, it needed to manage itself in a different way. The emphasis was on giving more empowerment and better team working. Information and the related management processes needed to reflect this new way of working. There would be greater visibility and transparency within the organization and managers would have more authority. It would bring together information about customers, departmental accounts and suppliers that had hitherto been separate.

Manoj, a senior manager in the company, undertook to establish this activity. He believed that since the user community (over 1000 people) were going to have to act and work differently, the project itself would have to be a model for the way that people would work.

To this end Manoj knew that he had to build a capability in the team and a strength of purpose in the vision which would be self-sustaining. A project like this would normally be allocated nine months to complete. Initially, he was given six weeks to build a system which would gain customer support, provide technical validity to the solution, gain the commitment of the teams who would be involved in its development and satisfy any critics of the project, team approach or technology. A matrix of twelve individuals from different departments and functions were to form the core part of the team.

The tangible result of this project was a 'product' – a piece of software; but it also gave a receptive customer base and a team which had the capability to continue to deliver rapidly. The team would have to acquire new technical skills, a keen understanding of the end goal and the ability to work in a different way. Manoj described it like this: 'You need to express your expectations of what you are going to achieve in a certain way so the team thinks in a certain way. Unless the team can think differently, there will be no learning, just output.'

Manoj understood that the key part in creating empowered teams was to ensure that they had a clear understanding and commitment to the outcome themselves. There would be no team if it did not have a shared purpose. The goal had to become real in their minds before it became a tangible result. It also had to align with their own personal goals. The team would have to learn new skills. Their efforts would not be centralized if they did not have an end in mind. Between one-third to one-half of the time was spent pacing the team's ideas, helping them work through their understanding of the end goal.

Clarity of outcomes meant that individuals would be free to make choices and decisions on behalf of the team. Instead of team members waiting for decisions (often on trivial matters like the colour of a screen) they were able to make real-time decisions. They understood the need to communicate both at fixed timeslots and in real time when the problems arose and had to be sorted immediately.

A communication room was set up. Instead of traditional project meetings, there were morning and evening meetings everyday where the team members briefed each other on progress. Roles were not fixed, e.g. designer or programmer, only the goal was fixed and people's natural skills and talents were employed by the team members to meet the needs of the individual team leaders. Individuals were encouraged to work in pairs where a leader owned the task or activity and the other person provided the support, testing or extra pair of hands as required. Team members realized their interdependence was crucial to the success of the project and the team became more and more self-managed as the project progressed.

Manoj paced the team, and was careful to manage their state. Team members were encouraged to spend social time together. The project has been very successful both from an organizational point of view and for the individuals involved. From the initial pilot, the system has been rolled out to over 1000 people since its inception. Team members have become more confident. The difference in their behaviours, talents, self-confidence and states is noticeable.

TO ERR IS HUMAN, TO FORGIVE MAY NOT BE COMPANY POLICY

Soon the team started to build up a feeling of ownership and responsibility. They were all capable and encouraged to make decisions within the framework of the shared outcomes. Responsibility carries the risk of making a mistake, which can be dangerous in an organization that has a 'blame culture'. When organizations do not tolerate mistakes and allocate responsibility only for mistakes, people will be paralysed. They will not risk anything, and they will seek ways to cover their tracks by passing the buck. They will refuse responsibility because it carries the risk of being wrong, and will not learn very much. Neither will the organization. When you always do what you have always done, you will always get what you have always got – this is the kiss of death in the present business climate. When the world moves fast, you need to keep up or you'll get trampled underfoot.

This old model of a blame culture was still alive in some members of the group; they were adept at covering their tracks. To err is human, but to forgive may not be company policy. A ritual existed whereby members of newly formed teams would send memos and record misgivings about team decisions in order to cover themselves if something went wrong later. They could say, 'I told you so' by pointing to the requisite e mail or memo. Manoj was aware of the old behaviours and clear about the ones he wanted to put in their place. He proposed that all communication should be face to face or by telephone. There was no e-mail or day-to-day procedural written documentation. Everyone was in the same boat.

Manoj also paid close attention to the emotional state of the team members. There was a briefing every morning at about 10.15, which gave everyone enough time to arrive at the office and settle in. This made for a much more productive meeting. When people are not in a good state they do not do such good work. He also gave the implicit message that their state was more important than the clock. The morning meeting was very focused. They broke the team outcomes into tasks for the day, every one was clear what they had to do, and they pressed on and did it. The project was a success in itself, the software was built in six weeks. It was also generative. In the wake of their accomplishment, team members are building project teams of their own, based on the model they experienced. Manoj took great pleasure in this. There were also follow-up workshops arranged to spread and consolidate the different ways of working.

APPRAISAL OR REPRISAL?

An appraisal system is a procedure that collects, checks, shares and gives information about employees. It can be used to improve their performance. It can be a tool for effective management, but it can just as easily amplify bad management, either by fanning the flames of discontent, or creating dissatisfaction when badly handled. Then appraisals become reprisals.

Appraisal can be a useful process where the person being appraised has a chance and a space to set and review their outcomes, and it is a good tool for tracking organizational, departmental and individual outcomes. It may also be used to assess potential and to estimate training and development needs.

Appraisal also has other possible uses:

O   To motivate staff to reach outcomes.
     An appraisal system in itself will not do this. It is just as likely to lead to demotivation, depending on how it is handled by the manager. Motivation comes from aligning tasks with the person's values. Furthermore, an appraisal often confuses judgement and motivation. To judge progress, compare where a person is now with where he started from, not with what others are doing. To motivate, ask the employee to compare where they are now with

their vision of an inspiring future, not your own or the organization's. Chapter 8 will examine motivation in detail.

O   To help to improve performance.
Appraisal is no substitute for regular feedback to the employee about how they are progressing from day to day, and week to week. It comes too late for the tasks that have been completed, and is too early for the tasks that are yet to come. Appraisal may be useful for assessing selection techniques. By reviewing the year you can see whether a person has performed as you would have predicted. It is feedback for you.

Performance appraisals are often used as a basis for promotion, a way of rewarding those who have done well in their old job, and because we think they are reliable indicators of future performance. Both these assumptions are questionable.

FROM LADDERS TO WALKWAYS

In traditional hierarchical organizations the career structure was like a ladder with fewer and fewer rungs, and your path led upwards. Moving up meant success, staying where you were was failure (ignoring for a moment the whole question of whether the ladder is up against the right wall). In flat organizations the ladders have become walkways. Appraisals can give information about what employees enjoy doing, what they value and the kind of area they like to work in, and this may be used as a basis for a move.

It does not follow that good performance in one job means good performance in another. Sometimes the opposite is true. The qualities needed to be a good salesperson are quite different from those needed to be a good sales supervisor, yet often the best sales people are rewarded by promotion to sales supervisor. Using appraisals for promotion can fuel the Peter Principle – that people are promoted to their level of incompetence. Work is accomplished by those who have yet to reach their level of incompetence.

It could be said that using appraisals as a basis for monetary rewards is a recipe for disaster. Reviewing goals, providing feedback and helping employees must be divorced from all consideration of rewards. It is hard to conduct an open and honest interview with the spectre of money hovering above the discussion. It also casts the manager in the uncomfortable and dubious role of being both coach and paymaster.

THE HEADTEACHER'S STUDY

Employees will dread appraisal time if it becomes an annual ritual where they are rated, berated and judged by criteria that do not seem to relate at all to the job they do. The nightmare begins with the necessary three-minute chat to 'put them at ease' before the manager goes through their faults in detail. This is like a recurring six-monthly nightmare of being back at school – a visit to the headteacher's study. Neither the employee, the manager nor the organization gains from it. If you were to take one measure of how well your appraisal system works we would advise you to consider: do the people (both managers and employees) come away from the appraisal interview feeling they have learned something and are energized and motivated? Or do they feel relief that it is over for another year, or have they simply gone through the motions and feel depressed and resentful?

APPRAISAL RULES

O   Appraisals are not a spectator sport – they should be conducted in privacy, with a mutually agreed, adequate amount of time to talk in detail.
O   The manager must have all the necessary information to hand before they start.
O   The manager must establish and maintain rapport using the skills of body matching and backtracking, as discussed in Chapter 2. Listening is the key. Whatever is said during that time, the employee must leave feeling that it has been a fair hearing. Use your second position skills. An employee is likely to be asking himself questions like: 'How am I doing?' 'Where am I going?' 'How can I improve?'
O   If you have criticisms, make them on the behavioural level and make them specific and descriptive. Describe the undesirable consequences. Ask for the employee's view. Agree a preferred course of action and the employee's commitment to it. When you praise, praise at each logical level – identity, values, skills, as well as behaviour.

An appraisal has four basic stages.

Deciding outcomes

There are three main areas, although they may overlap:

O   Work outcomes related to the organization. These are likely to be at the behaviour level.
O   Generative outcomes relating to management practice, increasing production, and optimizing relationships in the organization.
O   Personal development. These are capability and identity outcomes, and may involve learning new skills and attending training courses.

Thinking through outcomes

Appraisals do not work if the employee's outcomes are not well thought out. They are often too unspecific, not under control of the person, or have unforeseen consequences. Make sure all your people know how to set outcomes. It saves a great amount of time and effort.

Review

At agreed time periods, usually quarterly, the outcomes are reviewed by employee and manager to track the progress. Achieving outcomes is rarely a straight line. It is more like sailing – a series of zig zags. Appraisals are like a compass check to give feedback. Are we still on track? Mistakes are feedback for learning.

Learning and development from the results

Learning from the results may be formal or informal. You might ask:

> What would you do differently with the benefit of hindsight?
> Were there any unforeseen consequences?
> Did you overlook any significant resources?
> What have you learned as an individual?
> What have you learned as a departmental / team member?
> What have you learned about the organization?

A useful appraisal is a two-way process. When the employee is performing well, it is also a reflection on how well they are being managed (and vice versa). Many companies, e.g. Federal Express, BP and W.H. Smith, are also introducing upwards appraisals, where managers are appraised by employees. This can be carried out in a number of ways. Employees can fill out an anonymous questionnaire and the team evaluates the manager. Feedback sessions, action plans to implement feedback suggestions and, if necessary, counselling for the manager may follow. Remember, if it is not carefully handled, the recipient of upwards feedback, or indeed any kind of feedback, may experience the SARAH response:

> Shock, Anger, Rejection, Acceptance – Help!

At their best, appraisal schemes bring together all the important management skills – rapport, flexibility, setting outcomes, measuring performance and alignment on individual and company outcomes. When they work well, they can provide one means of translating the company purpose throughout the organization, and receiving feedback on how well it is working in practice.

DEVELOPING YOUR SKILLS

1   Examine your organization's mission statement, if it has one. What do you understand by it? How relevant is it to your work from day to day? How relevant is it to the work that goes on around you?

2   Consider some of the nominalizations you use and hear during the day. Notice your reaction. Do you assume you know what they mean? Do you know what they mean to others? When you use them to others, are you sure that they know what your meaning is? Unravel them when necessary by asking:

What is the action here?
Who is doing this?
What are they doing?
How are they doing it?

3   Consider any team projects that you are involved in.
Would every member of the team agree about the outcome?
Have you spent time together defining your outcome?
Are knowledge and resources easily available to all team members or are there information bottlenecks?

4   Consider your appraisal system. What are your outcomes when you appraise your people?
How do you know when you have achieved them?
Do your people know how to set and maintain outcomes?
Use rapport, pacing and leading, and backtracking skills in any appraisal interviews you conduct.

FURTHER READING

Bandler, Richard, and Grinder, John, *The Structure of Magic*, Science and Behaviour Books 1975.
Poundstone, William, *Prisoner's Dilemma*, Doubleday 1992.
Tichy, Noel and Sherman, Jack, *Control Your Destiny Or Someone Else Will*, Currency Doubleday 1993.
Virtuality Group plc, *Annual Report*, March 1994.

NOTE

1   Senge, Peter, Roberts, Charlotte, Ross, Richard, Smith, Bryan, and Kleiner, Art, *The Fifth Discipline Fieldbook*, Doubleday 1994.

6

ORGANIZATIONAL VALUES

❖

We have defined the organizational mission as how purpose and strategy interact. The mission statement points the way forward. There is still something missing – the values. These are as influential and pervasive in organizations as they are in individuals. All organizations embody values which inform its purpose, strategy and mission. This chapter explores how organizational values are expressed and how you can become aware of them.

MISSION IS NOT ENOUGH

Mission provides the destination and the route map. There is a growing awareness that mission on its own leaves out something important – values. Values provide the reason to make the journey at all. Values give the juice, the fuel for the journey. Values touch our emotions; we care about what happens. They make the mission come alive; they are the difference between mission and vision. Values are what make an organization tick – or explode.

Vision is the current hot topic with organizations, although it is not very clear what it means. It is a buzz word in empty space. We would like to propose a definition that we have found useful:

Mission + Values = Vision

Vision aligns people within an organization. It connects what people are doing and what is important to them, with what the organization wants to accomplish. Everyone in the company needs to know the vision, and also to feel they are part of it for this to happen. The best way of achieving this is to make everyone feel they have made a contribution; everyone needs to be consulted and have a say in a vision statement. Have you ever tried the experiment with a magnet and a jumble of iron filings on a sheet of paper? Shake the filings on to the paper. They fall randomly. Now put the magnet under the paper. The filings, as if by magic, are drawn into a pattern. The shared vision is the pattern and values are the magnet.

Companies and organizations consist of people coming together, acting together and sharing. Making them more effective is a group effort. Individualistic solutions like motivation will not work for organizational problems. Vision is the group equivalent of motivation.

All organizations have values whether they are aware of them or not. Vision only arises when they are integrated with the mission and transmitted throughout the organization. Values are often easiest to see from the customer viewpoint. Organizational values are the basis of key policy decisions. Management decisions are rarely clear cut and simple. There are no right answers, except perhaps in retrospect with 20/20 hindsight. Decisions are more concerned with balancing the different factors. What is the most important? The more uncertain the future, the more important the values as a guiding principle. Difficult decisions often show a clash of values. It is not that one way is right and the other is wrong, but each embodies different values. The vision statement embodies the most important values.

When we make a decision, that accords with our values, it feels right. When we go against our values it feels wrong. When an organization has a clear vision, making decisions becomes much easier; they feel right. This has a downside however. When you change your vision, or create one from nothing, decisions made on the old values will feel right, and those on the new values will feel wrong. What is more, organizations select people who feel comfortable with the current values whether explicit or implicit. Many cultural change programmes go astray because it is the people who are comfortable with the status quo that have to deal with the change. Change is likely to feel uncomfortable initially, which can be a signal that you are on the right track.

This chapter will deal with three aspects of organizational values and vision:

O   How can you find out your organization's values?
O   What happens if there is no alignment of values in an organization?
O   What is involved in creating a vision statement?

ORGANIZATIONAL VALUES MEAN NEVER HAVING TO WAIT FOR AN ELEVATOR

Organizational values are intangible and pervasive. They are like the background noise at a party – after a while you do not hear it any more, you just shout to be heard with everyone else. Some organizations are noisier than others.

The vision and values of an organization are likely to reflect the time when it was founded and the people who founded it. Lucky organizations find that these values are durable enough for it to continue to prosper.

An example of the endurance and power of values is seen in the Tylenol affair. Tylenol is the brand name used by the American company Johnson and Johnson for its widely used pain relief tablets. The values set in the 1950s by its president Robert Johnson still endure:

O   First, service to the customer.
O   Second, service to its employees and managers.
O   Third, service to the community.
O   Fourth, service to its stockholders.

Recalling these values, what would you do if some bottles of Tylenol were tampered with and several people died? Johnson and Johnson were serious about these values and committed to them. They recalled all the bottles. They lost a large amount of money in the short term, but in the long term they greatly enhanced their reputation, which may well have gained them more sales than they lost. Values are shown in action. There is only one thing worse than not knowing your values, and that is telling everyone what they are and then breaking them publicly.

Maintaining organizational values uses resources in unexpected ways, and may have absurd results – for example, the story about General Motors in Maryann Keller's book *Rude Awakening*. Whenever the General Motors assistant sales manager flew in from the central office in Kansas City, an executive was assigned to stand outside the door of his hotel until he arrived. Sometimes this involved a vigil in heavy snow, but the man had to be there to open the door when the manager arrived. GM had been known to buy the hotel elevator, to guarantee it would be free to take him to his room. Someone was assigned to stand outside his room all day on laundry duty. And he had to have his orange juice at a certain temperature every morning, so someone had to be on thermometer duty at breakfast time. These behaviours expressed values. GM may not have been clear exactly what values they expressed. To avoid being caught in such absurdities, they might have asked themselves three questions:

Do these actions truly express company values?
If they do, are there better ways of expressing company values?

Do they still connect with company values, or have they become an empty procedure?

WHAT IS YOUR METAPHOR?

In NLP, metaphors mean stories, comparisons, similes and analogies – they are always revealing. Metaphors are the quick way to find core organizational values. They often disclose more about an organization than any number of policy statements. The very words 'company', 'organization' and 'firm' began as metaphors:

○   The word 'company' is supposed to come from the Latin 'com panis' – the sharing of bread. People came together to share resources and formed a company.
○   The word 'firm' has a similar root to the word 'farm' and comes from the Latin 'firmare' to confirm.
○   Organization has the same root as 'organic' and 'organism' – a whole living system. The root of corporation is the Latin 'corporis' – a living body.

WHAT IS A METAPHOR FOR YOUR ORGANIZATION?

We ask this question in training. Here are some of the very interesting answers we have received:

A dinosaur
A brothel
A rottweiler
A headless chicken
An ivory tower
The Spanish Inquisition
A warm bath
A family
A private army
A jazz band
A premier division football team
An anthill
A tightrope
A circus

HEADLESS CHICKEN OR JAZZ COMBO?

Think of some current business metaphors. We have the corporate jungle – full of predators, bulls and bears. Jungle metaphors seem to proliferate in the stock market. Then there are the military metaphors (jungle warfare?). Business is war – 'Screw the opposition before it screws you'. We have corporate raiders, and business casualties. Sales is particularly rife with military talk. You marshal your arguments and take training courses to add ever more sophisticated weapons to your armoury of skills in your never ending battle with the competitors and even the customers. No wonder salespeople can suffer from battle fatigue. Sales organizations also use the metaphor of hunters and farmers – those sales people that go out and take new business, and those that cultivate accounts.

Tom Peters, in his book *Liberation Management*, makes much of business as fashion. Fashion is fickle; its only consistency is that it must change, and fast. Other similar metaphors are the organization as a network, a web, or a carnival, a jazz combo or a circus.

Organizations are compared to ladders. There are rungs up the ladder of success; you go higher and higher into the rarefied management air. And there is further to fall. We still live with a host of assumptions about organizations as a game of snakes and ladders – a step up is a reward, people want to climb the corporate ladder, and the ladder must go upwards. But many people want to stay where they are or take a step sideways. Microsoft is one company that recognizes this. An important part of keeping good people happy is a system where they can be promoted without having to go to the next management level if they do not want to. At Microsoft a good software developer can stay as a developer and still rise to the top tier of elite software 'architects'. These architects are company directors, and they report directly to Bill Gates on an informal basis. This gives them recognition, while keeping them in the work at which they excel. Many companies have similar systems where talented people who prove themselves in one area are given explicit recognition without being promoted beyond their level of competence.

The organization as a pyramid is a well known metaphor. Pyramids have small numbers of people on the top, supported by many at the bottom. (And it is not easy to balance on the top of a pyramid.) Thus the phrase, 'higher management'. Many firms are questioning the structure of the pyramid, arguing it should be turned upside down, so that the 'higher' management supports the base.

JUST WHEN YOU THOUGHT THE RAT RACE WAS OVER – ALONG COME FASTER RATS

Organizational structures reflect and create values. A metaphor creates a mind set; it predisposes people to think within certain limits. For example, if you are climbing a ladder, there may come a point where there are few rungs ahead of you, but many more behind you. Progress further up is difficult, and a climber may decide they have had enough. Their attention will then shift from climbing to not falling. This is the point when managers may consolidate, protect themselves, develop empires, make themselves indispensable by keeping hold of information, doing things 'by the book' and channelling their creativity into non-work areas. A pyramid or ladder structure will make this more likely. On the other hand, a ladder upwards can show a clear upward path that motivates people joining the company. We are not judging metaphors as good or bad; they are useful or not, depending on your outcome.

Metaphors have power, they are influential because they are so intangible and create a way of thinking. They are the clearest indication to the prevailing mental models that Peter Senge talks about in *The Fifth Discipline* – those ideas that are influential in the background of management thinking. Once this way of thinking and therefore acting is established it is hard to change. We become habituated and no longer notice what is there all the time. We were talking about this to a manager we know who told us a story about his childhood in India. He used to watch the tamed elephants and marvelled that, for such huge powerful animals, they never tried to escape; they were tethered only by a thin rope to a stake in the ground. The secret was revealed when he watched the adults train the young elephants.

The trainer would tie one of the elephant's feet to a stake in the ground. The young elephant was not very strong and try as he might, could not uproot the stake or break the rope. So he gave up. As the elephant grew strong he never tried again to break free, and so the result was that fully grown animals were restricted to a small area by a thin rope and a small stake.

What about the difference between a tight-rope and an escalator as a career path? Walking a tight-rope is difficult. It can also be dangerous (do you have a safety net?). One slip implies a big fall and it is hard to get back up again. It is likely to be stressful; you might suffer from vertigo and feel unbalanced. However it takes a great deal of skill and the rewards can be great. It also has some aspects of a public performance. People are watching and holding their breath. Will they succeed, or will they fall?

An escalator on the other hand is much more comfortable. You are moved forward without having to make any effort. You can even watch the world go by, and you will not travel any faster than anyone else on the escalator, unless you start climbing, using the momentum to speed your ascent.

Or do you feel caught in a rat race? A rat race is never over until you decide to stop racing.

MILITARY ACCOUNTING

Sometimes individual departments within an organization have their own dominating metaphors. A friend of ours was asked to do some team building with an accounting department that was spread over many different sites in a large organization. The problem was that the accounting department was out of step with the rest of the organization. When Duane met the team, the reason for the communication breakdown was obvious. The entire organization, following the lead of almost all the senior management throughout the country, used a military metaphor to describe their business. They spoke of killing the competition, waging war against the market and shooting from the hip. The accounting department, however, had no military experience and talked about debits, credits, collections and budgets. Duane spent an entire day translating their key activities and requests into military metaphors. Almost immediately communication was improved. As Duane said, 'We overwhelmed the defences, stormed the fortifications and led them to victory'. This is also a great example of pacing and leading.

The power of metaphors is that they channel our thinking in certain ways. They are more than a manner of speaking. They have consequences for thought and action, and how you treat people. Change your metaphor and you change the way you think.

A circle or a wheel is an organizational metaphor with growing support. A circle suggests 'central' management rather than 'higher' management. Charles Handy coined the phrase 'shamrock organization' in his book *The Age of Unreason* to describe a small, central core of people who run the company, with a number of links and networks to outside consultants, suppliers and business partners that are brought in as necessary for the project in hand.

Business as a ball game is a favoured metaphor. Teams engage other teams; there are goals and coaches; strategies that outflank the opposing team. The game metaphor is less brutal than the war metaphor. Other organizations started as a family business, and although they have grown, have kept the idea of an extended family. A family looks after its own, and demands loyalty as well.

Some managers and organizations favour a musical metaphor. 'Information technology', says Peter Drucker, 'is shifting the centre of gravity in employment from manual and clerical workers to knowledge workers who resist being told what to do by layers of middle management. These workers are more like instrumentalists.' They are professionals who enjoy working with other professionals. In an orchestra each group of musicians is equal but different. It is their difference that gives the richness and variety to the final piece. The role of the conductor is not to teach the musicians to be better players, but to get them to play together. The score is the mission statement, the interpretation is the vision. The CEO is the conductor of a symphony orchestra, and every player contributes to the complete effect.

STORY TIME

We hope you are starting to be curious about the metaphors that are active in your own organization. Here is a metaphorical quiz to help you explore your organization. Fill in the blanks. (There are no right or wrong answers.)

1 My organization is like . . .
2 Working in my organization is like . . .
3 Being promoted in my organization is like . . .
4 Our area of business is like . . .
5 Given these metaphors, what has to be true . . .
6 What are the implications of these metaphors?

THE VALUE OF VALUES - 10 BILLION DOLLARS

Management likes to quantify by money, and values have a cost as well as influencing resource allocation, as the General Motors elevator story illustrates. Organizational value-driven behaviour can be measured in monetary terms, although few companies do so. One of the challenges for management in the 1990s is how to measure these important 'soft' issues. They are very influential and are part of company assets in a real way – values have value.

In 1988 Philip Morris bought Kraft for nearly 13 billion dollars. What did this buy? The hard assets, the factories, offices, and warehouses were worth 1.3 billion dollars. The so called 'soft assets' were worth almost ten times the cost of the hard assets. Clearly these soft assets may not have showed up on Kraft's normal corporate balance sheet, but at the critical moment, they were very highly valued – at over *10 billion dollars*. Because soft issues are hard to quantify certainly does not mean they are worth nothing. Philip Morris bought over 10 billion dollars of brand equity, market positioning, creativity of the people at Kraft, and the organizational values that made all this possible.

Lest you think that the Kraft purchase was unusual, here are some more of the many examples of the value of intangibles. When Sterling Drug was acquired by Eastman Kodak in 1988 their book value of net assets was just over one billion dollars. Kodak paid over four billion dollars. When Bristol-Myers acquired Squibb in 1989 the book value of net assets was 1.5 billion dollars. Total price paid – over 12.5 billion dollars. The ratios are even higher in the service companies. When McCaw Cellular acquired Lin Broadcasting they paid 3.8 billion dollars for 209 million dollars' worth of tangible assets.

The ratio of a company's stock market value to the replacement value of its physical assets is known as *Tobin's q* after James Tobin, the Yale economics laureate. Several ratios were calculated in *Fortune* magazine in 1991. Microsoft had an 8:1 ratio of market value to physical assets value. Even hardware companies had ratios in the region of 2:1. The market puts huge value on creativity, intellectual capital, brand, image, and values – all those soft issues that rarely appear on balance sheets. The market is not sentimental; it values human imagination very highly. Do companies realize where their main value lies? How well is this precious quality managed? How is it increased?

ORGANIZATIONAL MYOPIA

Vision and values go hand in hand; they affect the lower logical levels of capabilities, behaviour and environment.

Vision is expressed in action

If a company is not aligned with the vision and does not express it through what it does, the vision is just empty words. Short sight will replace foresight. No organization is perfect, but watch for mismatches. A trainer friend of ours told us of the time she was called in to do some work at a training company that specialized in team building, particularly fostering trust between people. She began the day there and the time came for the mid-morning coffee break. They went to the staff room for a communal brew. Not only was the kettle chained to the wall, but so was the sugar bowl and even the teaspoon! This gave a message that clashed with the training course – it was a mismatch between values and environment.

A consultant we know was working with an international advertising agency, concentrating on their identity, beliefs and values, and giving communications skills training at the capability level. The company had a vision statement that emanated from their American office. Part of it was about giving their clients high value through creativity. The London office was engaged in a cost-cutting exercise and was considering salaries. They fired the two most expensive people in the agency – they were the most creative people they had, both had won several awards. The two found jobs in another firm almost immediately. This action gave the opposite message to the stated value.

Unless the vision is present throughout the organization, the business structures in place may not support the vision. For example, this same agency divided their work into three classes:

○   The rush jobs. Ideally they wanted to keep these to under 10 per cent of the total, because it did not give their designers time to produce creative solutions to the client's needs.

○   The normal work that gave the agency adequate time to produce a good solution. They aimed to place 65 per cent of work in this category.

○   The ideal situation where they had plenty of time to find a creative solution to the client's specification. They tried to put 25 per cent of their work in this category.

When they looked at the reality, the figures were very different. Sixty-five per cent of the work fell into the rush job category, 25 per cent in the normal category and only 10 per cent in the ideal category. They were caught in a spiral of urgent needs and satisfying unreasonable client requests. They could not meet their value of creative work in these circumstances. To take creativity seriously as a value, they had to change the way they worked. Aligning capability and behaviour with values means working in a way that expresses and supports those values.

REALIZING THE VALUES

Organizations demonstrate their values every day in the way they deal with their people and their customers. These values may have grown up from historical circumstances when the company was founded and from the personality of the founder. They may have grown haphazardly through the years, influenced by different managing directors, or they may have been consciously decided. We believe it is important that an organization is aware of its values. Values are the basis of procedures. You cannot manage effectively without shared values, and shared values are the basis of vision. Higher or central management manages the vision, acts as its custodian, creates the structures and procedures so they can be realized, and takes responsibility if it goes wrong. Senior management level should be driven by beliefs and values. An international survey in 1989 of 1,500 senior managers reported that a strong sense of vision is the quality most needed by a CEO.

How far should top management be involved in creating the vision? How is a vision statement created? There are four approaches to this question – Telling, Selling, Sharing and Creating. They are also management styles in their own right.

TELLING

This style uses the Nike slogan: 'Just do it'. Telling involves authority. You tell people what they are going to do. The implicit message is that you know best. This can be oppressive or paternal. The patron saint of this management style was Jack Welch of General Electric. He proclaimed that General Electric's businesses would be either number one or number two in their market or be sold. Anyone who disagreed was unlikely to last long in the company. This direct style requires power and credibility to work. The 'teller' must be clear, consistent, congruent, and open about the current reality. Telling works under crisis. It is probably the best method under extreme circumstances, when time is short and the pressure is on. When used constantly it can generate resentment and dependence, and can stifle creativity. Managers who rely on telling can feel frustrated when people do not do what they say. It is interesting that Jack Welch himself moved from a telling style to a more participative style.

We do not think that telling is the way to create a vision. A vision, if it is to be effective, should involve everyone. People must feel part of it, that is its power. To try to impose a company vision is a contradiction in terms, an attempt to have your cake and eat it. In our experience a vision statement is guaranteed not to work unless employees at all levels participate in the process.

SELLING

This style aims to make employees 'buy into' the organizational vision. The employees are the customers and the vision is the product. Selling vision is less directive than telling. You can point out the benefits of the values, and the consequences of not adopting them. Your rapport with your employees will be very important. Any sale depends on the relationship and trust between the parties. When there is no trust, there is no sale, whether you deal in used cars or vision.

The vision must offer the employees something specific that *they* value. 'This will allow us to decrease our expenses by 15 per cent' is hardly inspiring. 'You will have the responsibility to make decisions in your own area without interference' may be more motivating. You will want to gather feedback from both face-to-face interviews and from written questionnaires. This feedback must be confidential if you want it to be a genuine reaction.

SHARING

This approach is when management asks employees to act as consultants. Top management is still in charge of the vision but wants to hear every voice before deciding. Specific suggestions as well as vague ideas about the general direction are welcome. Management is still free to accept or reject what people say, just as they can with a consultant.

There are two dangers about this method. The first is that people might turn round and say, 'Don't ask us, isn't that your job?' This may show that people are feeling disempowered, and perhaps believe that whatever they say it is not going to be considered. It can happen if you switch abruptly from a telling mode to a sharing mode without adequate pacing. In this situation, do not demand answers, but look carefully at the whole organizational history, values and structures that have led you to such a sorry state. You could begin by pacing, by saying: 'Yes, I know in the past we have not listened to your views as much as we could have, but now we are genuinely interested'. This will not be credible unless it is accompanied by other actions that act as convincers. Management will need to consult with the people on other subjects and act on what they say. Also, it must be done congruently and success will depend to a large extent on your personal credibility and communication skills.

The second danger is that of becoming paralysed by the diversity of views, and thinking perhaps that you must try and please everybody. The result could be a compromise that pleases nobody. People feel strongly about values. Remember that different viewpoints are literally that, points of view; none contains the whole truth. Management is still responsible for fashioning a vision from these multiple perspectives.

There are many ways to gather people's views. Small teams work well, perhaps starting with higher management and then cascading down the organization. Each member of one team forms another team around them and continues the process. Viewpoints can be gathered anonymously or in open meetings, and the results should be available at any time so everybody can see that progress is being made. Even here, there is the presupposition that vision and values are created 'at the top' of the organization. In the telling mode it is pushed downwards. In the selling mode it is sold downwards and in the sharing mode it cascades (or trickles) downwards.

CREATING

The creative style is the most difficult but most rewarding to manage. It takes a great deal of trust initially for management to initiate this process. It is by far the least common, and is one of the skills that Senge identifies as making a learning organization. It involves every member of the organization in the creative process, and dispenses with the idea that higher management knows best. This process starts with each individual defining their personal vision as best they can. What is important to them? This does not lead to anarchy, as one might expect, for people do not come to work wanting the organization to fail, or to do a bad job. They do the best they can given the circumstances they are in. When the organization is oppressive, they just try to get by. Part of creating a vision is creating an organization to which everyone wants and is proud to belong.

Once everyone has articulated their personal vision, then teams are formed to bring these ideas together. The results from the team discussion travel with equal speed and weight both up and down the organization. Everyone is equal. Everyone has a voice. There is no taking samples of people's views in the hope that they will be representative. Everyone does not have to agree, in fact they rarely will. Disagreement will show up people's beliefs about themselves and the organization and lead to better understanding of both. The process is a powerful one and must itself become part of the resulting vision. Creating values and vision in this way is a huge subject and this is merely to scratch the surface. *The Fifth Discipline Fieldbook* is a good source of information and ideas about the process.

TIME TRAVELLING

These are the some of the questions to ask in teams when creating a vision. Imagine yourself into the future, one year, three years, five years, whatever time span you want to consider. You are happy. You have created the organization you wanted to create. From this vantage point ask yourself:

IDENTITY

What does our organization look like?
How are we perceived, what is our image?
What role do we have in the community?
How do we advertise ourselves?
What single sentence would we want our customers to say about us?
What is our metaphor?

BELIEFS AND VALUES

What are our values?
How do we reward people?
What security do we have?
What do we believe about our people?
What do we believe about our customers?

CAPABILITY

Who are the stakeholders in this organization?
How do we produce value for them?
How do we make money?
What profits are we making?
What is our turnover?

BEHAVIOUR

What products or services are we selling?
How do the various parts of the company relate together?
What do we feel about working for this organization?

ENVIRONMENT

How large is the organization?
Where is it located?

How big is our workforce?
How do we communicate?

WHERE ARE YOU?

Although we have concentrated on the four modes of telling, selling, sharing and creating in terms of organizational values, they are also general management styles. Do you recognize your own preference? There is no right and wrong way. In some situations telling is the best way to manage people. Sometimes you may sell your ideas, or share them. On some occasions, perhaps when building a team for the first time, you will be creating. It is very powerful when you create something together that everyone feels they own. Remember pacing and leading works, whichever style you adopt. If you are telling or selling, take people's reservations into account and acknowledge them. If you have used mostly telling and selling, then people will be reluctant to open out in a sharing or creating way. You will need to pace this reluctance.

You will also need to manage upwards. Your manager may expect you to help him or her tell or sell their vision. Understand their position. Pace their reality and find out what they are trying to do. Understanding your own values and other people's values as a basis of vision is the key to influence and ultimately leadership. Vision is simple, but not easy.

DEVELOPING YOUR SKILLS

1   What are the main values of your company? How are they expressed?
2   Ask both employees and customers to tell you what they see as the main organizational values. If you have a vision or mission statement, do they know what it is? (Do you?)
3   What are the metaphors current in your organization? Is it like a team? A family? An army? A brass band? Or what?
4   What does the current predominant metaphor presuppose? Is this useful?

FURTHER READING

Keller, Maryann, *Rude Awakening*, William Morrow 1989.
O'Connor, Joseph, and Seymour, John, *Training With NLP*, Thorsons 1994.

Peters, Tom, *Liberation Management*, Macmillan 1992.
Senge, Peter, et al., *The Fifth Discipline*, Doubleday 1990.
Stewart, Thomas, *Fortune*, 3 June 1991.
Tichy, Noel, and Sherman, Jack, *Control Your Destiny Or Someone Else Will*, Currency Doubleday 1993.

7

INDIVIDUAL VALUES

❖

Outcomes are what you want. Values are why you want what you want. Corporate values fuel corporate vision. Our individual values are the basis of our motivation and the choices we make. They are those things that are important to us. Values are usually abstract words, nominalizations such as love, happiness, achievement, ambition, health and fun. Values invoke emotions. The words may be abstract, but the feelings behind them are not. In NLP, the word 'criteria' is often used instead of values. Criteria are values applied to a particular context like work. You are likely to have different values in different situations, for example, what is most important to you at work, and what is most important to you on holiday are probably different. One of your values in choosing a car could be safety; in choosing your work, challenge could be the main value.

This chapter will help you to explore your own values and those of your colleagues. Our values strongly influence our decisions. Organizational values influence corporate decisions. Your values may clash with or complement the organizational values. It is extremely uncomfortable to work in an organization that embodies radically different values from your own. You will constantly feel incongruent. A decision for both individuals and corporations is often difficult because it involves a choice between fulfilling two values; there is no right and wrong, just good and not so good.

To maximize your influence upwards, downwards and horizontally in the organization, you must also find out the values of your colleagues. This is also the key to leadership. There are three facets of values that we would like to explore:

○   How you prioritize your values. Some are more important than others. When it comes to a choice, you will act to fulfil the higher one.

○   The different types of values. Some we are attracted towards – love, friendship, respect, responsibility, fun and safety. Others we want to avoid – rejection, loneliness, failure and guilt. Sometimes it is a matter of emphasis, for example whether we move towards acceptance or away from rejection.

○   How you know your values are being honoured or violated. We have rules about what has to occur for our values to be fulfilled. Specific behaviours let us know our values are being met, or violated.

WORKING VALUES

What is important to you in your work? Think about the following questions and write down the answers:

> What three things help you do your job well?
> Why are they important to you?
> What three things do you like about your job?
> Why are they important to you?
> What does this suggest about the sort of person you are?
> When you retire or leave this job what will you have wanted to have achieved?
> What would it have been like not to have achieved it?
> How will those things that you like about your job help you to achieve this?

You will see from these answers what you value about your work, and what you do not like. The next step is to establish how you rank your values in order of importance.

HIERARCHY OF VALUES

Your values will in part depend on your circumstances, as Maslow's hierarchy of needs emphasizes. The most basic are the physiological needs such as hunger, thirst and sleep. We have to fulfil these basic needs first. We hardly worry about self-actualization if we are starving, because unless we eat some food, there will be no self to actualize. Next are the needs for safety and security, then the social needs of acceptance, affiliation, friendship and love. Given that these basic needs are satisfied, we move into the realm of self-esteem, self-respect, achievement and recognition. Lastly there are those needs that Maslow called self-actualization – personal development and growth, developing one's full potential.

When you are adequately fed, clothed and housed, your values are likely to comprise affiliation, self-esteem and self-actualization and you will rank them in order of importance. Social and cultural factors come into play here. In the US and Britain a survey found that the top values were: family happiness, economic security, health, ambition and fulfilment. Recently a friend of ours did some consulting in Russia. She found that in a group of Russian business people, freedom was far and away the most important value. None of the others had any meaning without freedom. In the US and Britain such basic freedom is taken for granted, not in Russia.

Work is an important way we can fulfil many of our values. The money we are paid helps to satisfy our basic physiological and security needs, and we also look to our work to satisfy other needs and values such as friendship and recognition, even personal development and growth.

You can find out how you rank your values very simply. Pick a context where you want to know your value hierarchy. We will take work as an example.

1   Think of two or three important experiences in your work. Write down some key phrases about each experience. What did you gain from it? How did you feel about it? What did you learn from it? What did it enable you to avoid?

2   Take each phrase and ask yourself: 'What is important to me about that?' You will soon have a list of about a dozen words. From all the words you have written pick the five that are the most important to you.

3   Now, if you had to lose one, which would it be? You do not lose it really of course, the one you pick comes bottom of this list. Of the four that are left, if you had to lose one which would it be? Continue until you have only one left. That is your highest value in the context of work.

You have now established a series of values about your work in ascending order of importance. Certain values have to be met for you to continue working. There will be a connection between your values at work and those in other areas of your life. Work and family values may clash; for example, some people leave a job when it takes them away from their family for extended periods.

Now you have established your most important working values, ask yourself, 'What can I do to ensure that these are met in my work?'

Think about the values of your organization, either explicitly stated, or what you perceive them to be. How do they match up with your values? Do they align, or are they seriously mismatched?

Next, from the point of view of the organization, ask yourself:

How am I valuable to the organization?
How am I important in maintaining the environment of the organization?
What do I do that the organization values?
What skills do I have that the organization values?

POSITIVE INTENTION – THE DEVIL'S ADVOCATE

Good managers will deal with problem behaviour from the point of view of values. Rather than simply challenging the behaviour, they make it clear that the behaviour is unacceptable while pacing and acknowledging the values behind it. Behaviour is purposeful. We always act to achieve something that is important to us, something we value. Unfortunately, the actions or behaviour may not be a very good way of achieving it and may cause trouble for others. For example, a manager we know was having trouble with one member of his team. This person would constantly challenge the thoughts and proposals of other members. He played the devil's advocate, finding faults with details. This became very wearing. The other members of the team started to resent him. One of them said: 'I would not feel so bad if he contributed something positive every now and then, but it is always so negative.' This person's behaviour was destroying team rapport, yet his area of expertise was important and he could not be replaced in the current project.

We suggested the manager take this man aside, ask him what he wanted to achieve through his questioning, and why this was important to him. It turned out that he valued safety very highly. A project in his previous job had ended in disaster, because plans were not properly checked, and crucial details were left out. The company lost a great deal of money. He vowed this would never happen again in any work he was engaged on. 'I want the plan to be absolutely foolproof in every detail' was how he expressed it. Safety and accuracy of detail were very important to him and our friend shared these values and said so. Now came the $64,000 question. 'Is your constant challenging effective?' The answer was no. The other team members were not paying attention to his contribution; they were not listening but paying him lip service only in their attempt to move on. This made him more nervous and he challenged all the more. The manager suggested that he had a very useful role as devil's advocate of the group, but should wait until plans were more fully formulated before asking for details. He agreed.

After that the group's effectiveness was greatly increased. The others knew that they had the space they needed to develop plans and they had better be good ones. Challenges came later and were more constructive, and very valuable. Several small improvements were made that improved the project's cost efficiency. Our friend paced the man's values and utilized them for the benefit of the group.

In NLP it is presupposed that people have a positive intention for what they do: they are trying to achieve something of value for themselves. What they do to achieve it may seem bizarre or annoying. We are all different and see the world in different ways; we do not really know what others are trying to achieve. We do not see their action from their point of view unless we make an effort to go to second position with them. In the same way others do not see our actions from our point of view. Their understanding can be very different from our intention. In NLP there is a saying: 'The meaning of the communication is the response it gets.' This is a way of saying, look at your actions and words from the other person's point of view as well as your own. When what you say or do does not achieve the desired response, find out what has happened and say or do something different until you receive the response you do want.

MONEY

Money may well have figured among your values in the last exercise. Money has no worth in itself, it makes other values possible. It is a means to an end, it buys things you want, both tangible and intangible, for example: recognition, freedom, safety, comfort, holidays, and cars. Money is important, and it is particularly annoying being told it isn't by someone who has an abundance of it. However, money is an overused and overestimated incentive.

HOW IMPORTANT IS MONEY?

In the many surveys carried out to find what motivates people in business, money hardly ever comes first. In a survey of over 50,000 utility company applicants over a period of thirty years, pay came sixth out of ten job factors. However, when asked what they thought *other* people thought was important, most people picked pay. Other surveys show similar results. It is interesting that while we do not rank

> pay as the most important value for ourselves, we overestimate its
> importance for others.

In a study of career development of 2000 people in middle to top
management by Nigel Nicholson and Michael West, the top four reasons for
changing jobs were:

1   To do something more challenging and fulfilling.
2   A step towards career outcomes.
3   To change career direction.
4   To improve their standard of living.

This does not support managerial job hopping in search of higher salaries.
One finding in the survey was worrying. Three times as many managers
pursued these values by changing companies than by internal promotion.
Do organizations recognize these values? The figures suggest that often the
answer is no, organizations are not pacing their people. So how can they
provide work that is challenging and fulfilling?

The first way is by having a structure that allows people to do different
types of work. Goal-focused project teamwork is excellent. The projects
keep changing, and people are constantly challenged to master different
tasks. On the other hand, a functional job may seem challenging and
fulfilling at the start, but once mastered, it becomes repetitious.

The second way is through you, their manager. Give them work that is
challenging. How do you know what that is? Simple. Ask. Often managers
assume what they or the organization find challenging and fulfilling is so for
everyone. Given that certain tasks have to be completed, let the people do
it in their own way, that is most fulfilling for them. Once again the message
is to manage from a values base and not a behavioural base. You can play
to a person's weakness. Give tasks that will develop the person as well as
let them do what they do well. Doing an unfamiliar task involves learning.
Doing a familiar task that you are already good at involves little learning, if
any. Give support at the same time as you give responsibility. Make sure
they understand that if they get into difficulties they know who to ask for
help.

Organizations meet the fourth value – to improve the standard of living –
appropriately enough with money. However, people will take money as a
substitute for other things they really want, but are not receiving, such as:
promotion, respect, recognition, or status. And they will take a large amount
of it as compensation – too much of what you do not want is still not
enough.

PEANUTS AND GOLDEN BANANAS

Money is often given as a form of recognition, a point neatly illustrated by the legend of the IBM golden banana. The story is that Tom Watson, when he was chairman of IBM, would write out a cheque on the spot as a reward for any person who impressed him with a good idea that he could adopt. One day a person came into his office with an excellent idea. Watson was pleased. He rummaged in his desk for his cheque book, but found only a banana. Rising to the occasion, he handed it over. From that moment, the legend of the golden banana was born and the most coveted award at IBM was a gold pin in the shape of a banana.

Although money is not always an incentive, a poor or manifestly unfair monetary reward is a great disincentive. If you pay peanuts, all you employ are monkeys. Or perhaps it is better to say by paying peanuts you give people the message that they are only monkeys, and therefore they will live down to your expectations.

Because lack of money can demotivate does not mean, however, that the more money, the more motivation. People at work are more concerned about money if they are not making what they consider to be enough. Man lives for bread alone when there is very little bread to be had. Some people are less concerned about the level of their earnings than whether it is a fair day's pay for a fair day's work, in other words they are driven more by the value of fairness or justice, than by riches. Others are more concerned that their level of pay reflects their seniority.

MONEY AS A WAY OF MEASURING VALUES

You can use money as a way of measuring what you value about your work. Go back to the things you value about your job that you noted down from the questions earlier in this chapter. What extra financial bonus would you want to compensate you for a job that does not fulfil each of those values? The bigger the bonus, the higher ranked the value. Some values may be priceless.

Here are some questions that can clarify how money relates to your value hierarchy.

What yearly salary would make you feel financially secure?
What is the difference (if any) between this and the salary you have now?
If there is a shortfall, what values do your work satisfy that are more important to you than the feeling of financial security?

RULES ABOUT VALUES

We have rules about what has to happen in order for our values to be fulfilled. Suppose you value recognition in your work. How do you know when you have been recognized? What does it mean on the level of *behaviour*? The specific behaviours that let you know your values have been met are called *criterial equivalents* in NLP. They are evidence of our values being met. For some people it might be a word of praise, others want to be recognized in print, for others it means a salary rise.

Criterial equivalents are fascinating. Many people put a value on friendship for example, but if you ask different people, 'How would you know someone is a friend?' you will hear several different answers. One person we know replied without thinking, 'He would always arrive on time.'

We asked many people to complete the sentence: 'A friend is someone who . . .' and heard some very varied answers.

> 'I could trust to do something for me at short notice, even if I could not explain why.'
> 'Would tell me if I had bad breath.'
> 'Someone who would take me in if the police were after me.'

We also have rules about what has to happen for our values to be violated. A manager we know carried through a very successful and ground-breaking project from start to finish, planning, bringing the team together, giving them a vision of what they could accomplish, and delivering the results to the organization on time. While everybody congratulated him to his face, when the results were written up for a national newspaper, he was not mentioned. His manager was. This violated his values of respect and recognition so much that he started looking for another job.

In some organizations size of desk or office is a criterial equivalent of recognition. We have known some where these environmental tokens are exactly graded. Your entitled area of office is exactly specified, the size of desk, the grade of carpet, right down to how many pictures you may have on your wall. For some managers, the criterial equivalent of productivity is a desk groaning with paperwork. When they see this, it is evidence for them that the person is busy and therefore productive. Busyness and productivity are not related of course, but such value rules are not logical. Status is shown by an overloaded in-tray. In other organizations an overloaded in-tray is evidence of being disorganized.

Managers make decisions about applicants at job interviews on the basis of their value rules. There is the old school tie. Some managers are impressed, others may feel the applicant is trying to impress with who they know rather than with what they know. Smoking violates many people's values. One manager we know will immediately stop an interview if the candidate is a smoker.

We have found some interesting value rules for competence. Some people know they are competent at a task when they have done it once. Others are not sure until they have done it two or three times. Others never truly feel they are competent. They continue to credit their success to the environment or behaviour. In other words, they feel lucky, or other people helped them, or it was a one-off result. Others claim competence when they feel they can do it if they put their mind to it. They may never actually have done it.

Job security is an important value. Many people need employment to feel secure. Some people will only feel secure if they have a guaranteed job for life, and these jobs are very few and far between. Others only need to feel they are employable.

How do you judge creativity? For some it means coming up with a new idea, something that no-one else has thought of before. For others it means being able to synthesize different ideas into a coherent whole that is more than the sum of its parts. There are many types of creativity. Our values become real when they are connected to real actions in the real world.

The rules we have for our values to be fulfilled may be disempowering. There are three ways that they can make life difficult for you and others:

○   They are impossible to meet. When your values are so exactly specified or unusual that they are unlikely to be met, then you have set yourself up for disappointment.

○   You have no control over the situation. If you want your values to be met regularly, then you need to play an active part. You do not have to change or give up your values, but consider changing your rules so you gain more direct influence over how they are fulfilled.

○   Your rules are disempowering if you have many for how your values can be violated and few for how they can be fulfilled. If this is so, you have set up a situation where you have many ways to feel bad and few ways to feel good.

You may also want to explore your values and rules in other fields. What do you value about relationships? Working life is made of them. What is important to you about personal relationships? Of those values that are important to you: How do you know when they have been met? How do you know when they have been broken?

VALUES IN ACTION – SUMMARY

We believe that values are one of the most underrated yet most influential factors for managers. Values drive organizational behaviour.

O   Is the organization aware of its values?
O   Have these values been consciously chosen?
O   What are the rules for fulfillment of the organizational values?

We would like to discuss value rules at an organizational level – evidence that its values are being met. Organizations spend a great deal of time and effort on statistical measurements in quality programmes to ensure that what they sell is up to specification, and rightly so. The setting and adherence to value standards receives less attention. It is less easy to do. There is no reason why both sorts of standards cannot be addressed. Ideally, products meet quality standards which are well specified. In the same way, the organization should have a set of values that are also well specified, and determine not only how it deals with its customers but also how it treats the people who work there. When an organization is aligned, the same values are used in treating its employees as treating its customers. Customer care and employee care go hand in hand. Inadequately cared for employees will find it hard to adequately care for customers.

A consultant we know had been called into a charity that wanted help in restructuring. It had grown a great deal in a few years and needed to plan a long-term strategy. The first step was to spend two days working on its values and mission. Once the core values were defined, the strategies, the process and the action plan were all defined in terms of rules – what had to be true for these values to be manifest in the organization. The values and strategy were aligned – this charity had a vision. It does not work well to go the opposite way – to bolt the values onto a pre-existing strategy and action plan; the values will be distorted and the result is unlikely to be convincing.

Organizations can easily make rules for values like customer care. One example is Delta Dental Plan of Massachusetts, a medical insurance company. In 1990 they instituted a very specific guarantee of service excellence. Here are four of the points.

O   If a client company does not make a 10 per cent annual saving on dental fees, Delta will refund the difference.
O   If a customer's enquiry cannot be answered on the spot someone will return the call within twenty-four hours or Delta will pay the client 50 dollars.
O   All claims are accurately processed within thirty days, or Delta remits the client one month's administration fee, which can run into thousands of dollars.

O   Delta delivers its clients' reports by the tenth of each month or pays
        the client 50 dollars.

Delta accept responsibility for these values by taking the initiative in making
payments, even when the client does not complain. They also link the
values, thresholds and projects to continuously improve services and learn
from mistakes. Procedures have been instituted where a quality co-
ordinator reviews every reported problem, analyses the cause and proposes
corrective action. This has led to market success. In the middle of 1992,
sales leads were up by half and customer retention was at 98 per cent.
    Delta involved key customers in their planning, asking them what
services were most important to them, how the guarantees would work, and
the size of the payouts offered. Delta paid great attention to their customers
both with their guarantee and the way they arrived at it.
    Understanding your own values, and how they align with the organiza-
tional values will determine how satisfying you find your work. Understanding other people's values is the key to motivation and leadership.
Usually we do not understand other people's values and try to convince
them on the basis of our own. We try to argue with them as if they believed
as we believe, and that the same things are important to them as they are to
us. If this were so, there would be no argument and no need to convince.
You would have perfect agreement. We spend much of our lives giving
what we wish to receive. When you take your people's values into account
you come close to putting your management skills where they can make a
real difference – at the level of human imagination.

DEVELOPING YOUR SKILLS

1   Listen to the value words that people use. They will mostly be
        nominalizations – abstract nouns. You cannot know exactly what
        they mean without asking.
2   Find out what is important to you about your work, and prioritize
        those values. How does your company help you attain those
        values? How does it hinder you? What more can you do to realize
        those values in your work?
3   Next time a person behaves in a way that is a problem, think about
        the positive intention behind their actions. If appropriate, ask
        them.
4   Complete the following sentences, and ask your work colleagues to
        do so as well: 'A motivated person is someone who . . .' 'A
        committed person is someone who . . .'

FURTHER READING

Cohen, Paul, 'Change the Rules of Your Industry's Game with an Ironclad Guarantee', *On Achieving Excellence* magazine, August 1991.

Kotter, John, and Haskett, James, 'The Caring Company: a Review of Corporate Culture and Performance', *The Economist*, 6 June 1992.

O'Connor, Joseph and McDermott, Ian, *Principles of NLP*, Thorsons 1996.

Peters, Tom and Waterman, R., *In Search of Excellence*, Pan 1982.

Phillips, Michael, and Rasberry, Salli, *The Seven Laws of Money*, Random House 1974.

8

THE MOTIVATIONAL MINEFIELD

❖

Is it part of a manager's job to motivate people? If so, how?

Let us clarify some assumptions behind these questions. Does motivation come from the outside or inside? What is motivation anyway? What do you see, hear and feel when someone is motivated?

IS MOTIVATION A DORMITIVE PRINCIPLE?

In 1654 the French playwright Molière wrote a comedy in which a panel of learned doctors were investigating the reason why opium makes people sleep. After carefully considering the question, they came to the conclusion that opium made people sleep because it contained a 'dormitive principle'. This sounds grand, but all it says is that opium puts you to sleep because it contains something that puts you to sleep. Molière had little sympathy for doctors, but here he poked fun at a common characteristic – making a word into an explanation.

The word 'motivation' is a nominalization – an abstract noun, frozen in time, representing a process. It is a trap to ask about the qualities of motivation. What is the process behind the word? It is a combination of circumstances that accord with our values that moves us to act. Such circumstances can come from without (extrinsic motivation), or from within the person (intrinsic motivation). 'Motivation' and its sister word 'commitment' risk becoming 'dormitive principles' if they are used to explain what they describe. Do people need extrinsic motivation and, if so, what works? What moves people?

Traditionally, and simplistically, there are two approaches to moving people from without: the carrot and the stick. The carrot approach is to

121

reward people for their efforts. The stick method says no – people want to avoid pain, so threaten them with unpleasant consequences for not moving. The selling profession harbours the purest examples of both schools of thought. The carrot approach is to have league tables of sales people, Caribbean cruises and rewards for being 'salesperson of the month'. The extreme stick approach is summed up in the story of the manager who gathers all his sales people together on Monday morning and tells them, 'I am firing you all now. You have until Friday to persuade me to give you your jobs back.'

THE FLOGGING WILL CONTINUE UNTIL MORALE IMPROVES

Stick management is often strikingly ineffective in the medium and long term because it rarely succeeds in encouraging creativity and innovation.

A COOKING METAPHOR FOR STICK MANAGEMENT

Here is an experiment you can carry out that is an excellent metaphor for the long-term effects of stick management. Lightly grease the floor of a microwave oven with sunflower oil. Place as many grapes as there are employees on one side of the oven. Close the door and place your bets on the winning grapes. Push the start button. The physics of heat transfer make the grapes skate across the hot oil. Some high achieving grapes will skate far and fast. They will then explode due to the same physics of heat transfer.

Both grapes and people burn out if the temperature becomes too high.

Punishment may work to *stop* people doing things, but this is not motivating them to actively move in the direction of continuous improvement. They may or may not do better next time. They will certainly want to avoid mistakes and therefore avoid risk as well. Sometimes it seems as if punishment does lead to improved performance, but this is not cause and effect, just statistics. The statistical principle of regression means that over a period of time any event tends to approach a middle value – events average out. If the weather is spectacularly bad one day, it is more likely to improve than deteriorate the next. Very good weather will probably not last, because if it did it would be normal, and therefore not noteworthy. Any climate has a mean value between its two extremes, so extremes are likely to be followed by a movement towards the mean. In the same way, shareholders are likely to be disappointed after a superb year, dividends are rarely equal or higher the next year. Predictions and decisions based on extremes will usually be wrong.

So we would expect a poor performance to be followed by a better one on the regression principle, regardless of punishment. The punishment may have as much effect on performance as a rain dance in improving the weather. Also, rewards may be given after a very good performance. The regression principle means that this is likely to be followed by a less good performance, and reward may thus seem ineffective.

'Stick' management motivates people to do one thing – avoid the stick.

THE CARROT PROBLEM

Most motivational schemes are based on the carrot approach – exceptional performance is rewarded. This is the basis of all bonus schemes, financial and other incentives. It seems reasonable to reward in order to thank someone for good work above and beyond the call of duty. There is a strong argument, however, that rewards motivate only in very limited circumstances, and can even be counterproductive.[1]

Surprisingly, research over the last twenty-five years has found no evidence that people work any more productively when they are expecting to be rewarded for their performance, than when they are expected to be rewarded equally or on the basis of need.[2] The only exception is when the task is very easy, and there is no inherent satisfaction in performing it. Give a person a simple, repetitive task and he will probably do it faster if paid extra for doing so. He will not necessarily do it better. Rewards are least effective when the task is challenging or needs creative thought. There is no correlation between the money paid to creative people and the quality of their work. Productivity does not follow pay, it is the opposite:

> The best creative people get the best money, the money is paid for talent and results, not to motivate them.

The works of Deutsch, Kohn[3] and McGraw contain overwhelming evidence that motivation by reward is more complex than it seems and mostly ineffective. Reward and effort are connected, but measurement over time refutes the claim that we can make people work harder or better by incentive alone. The problem with incentive pay is that it treats people in a mechanistic way, and people do not react in predictable ways. They adapt, change and work out how to use such systems for their own ends. The available research also indicates that people who are offered rewards choose easier tasks. They often work harder, but the work is of lower quality and less creative than the work done by people who were not rewarded for working on the same problems.

A CAUTIONARY TALE

In 1947 a shepherd boy wandering in the hills beside the Dead Sea found a number of large clay jars in a cave. Inside the jars were scrolls – a remarkable archaeological find, now known as the Dead Sea scrolls. These were the teachings of a Jewish religious sect, written 1000 years earlier than any previously found material. They had been hidden in the caves from the Romans. Archaeologists throughout the world were amazed and delighted. They hoped there were more scrolls, and naturally wanted to find everything possible. They offered incentives – the more pieces of parchment you found, the more money you received. So the enterprising locals took the scrolls from the jars and tore them into thousands of fragments with the result that there are now over 10,000 pieces of parchment, and huge confusion about which fragments belong together.

Motivating needs to be disentangled from two other issues. First, it is not concerned with judging progress. Comparing yourself with others who are doing better is not motivating, but demoralizing, especially if you have no way of closing the gap. When there is nothing you can do, or are allowed to do, you will simply feel powerless.

Secondly, people feel they deserve a fair financial reward for their work. While more money may not motivate, perceived unfair remuneration is a main cause of dissatisfaction, resentment and loss of interest. We are certainly not arguing against fair financial reward. Given that people are fairly rewarded we are saying that extra reward and bonuses are not only ineffective but sometimes have the opposite effect to the one intended. They can be demotivating for the following reasons:

O   The rewards on offer are not what the person values. Most rewards are financial, and as we have seen, contrary to widespread belief, money does not usually feature in most people's top three values. Offering a person something they do not value is not motivating. A reward is only as valuable as the recipient thinks it is. It is rare indeed for anyone in management to take the trouble to find out what is important to a person. (When did someone last ask you?) When you do not know what a person values, you do not know what they want or what motivates them.

○ Rewards can turn out to be punishments. Both rewards and punishments come from the same basic view of manipulating behaviour. You may remember a time when you or your colleagues expected a reward and then it failed to materialize. Can you remember how you felt? Most people report feeling angry and demoralized. Thus reward schemes can also produce punishments by creating the possibility of not receiving them.

○ Rewards can sour relationships, and frequently do nothing to foster co-operation and collaboration in teams. In particular, occasions where rewards are scarce, and only one person or team can win, create strife rather than co-operation. Other people become obstacles, not resources. Many organizations rank employees against each other or give a bonus to an entire department. This can lead to intense peer pressure throughout the department; one person's mistake can lose the reward for everyone. It is the strategy of the primary school teacher who promises a treat at the end of the day only if everyone is good. If the bonus does not materialize, who is to blame? There will be a scapegoat. Scarce rewards guarantee strife and hostility.

○ Rewards ignore the causes behind behaviour. When a person is working very well, you want to know how – so you can model them and teach others what they are doing. They may be exceptionally creative, in which case extra rewards will either be irrelevant or demotivating. They may be favourably placed in the system and they may be benefiting from factors that are completely outside their control. (Others may be penalized by the same factors.) W. Edwards Deming has called the system of rewarding merit through appraisal 'the most powerful inhibitor to quality and productivity in the Western world . . . it nourishes short term performance, annihilates long term planning, builds fear, demolishes teamwork, nourishes rivalry . . . and leaves people bitter'.[4] He also says it is unfair to hold people responsible for systemic factors that are beyond their control. Such factors are liable to be very influential and go unnoticed in a large organization.

○ Rewards encourage and reinforce what has succeeded in the past so they may discourage experiments and possible better procedures. People working for rewards tend to work for success at the task, rather than to learn from it. In creative problem solving, the wrong answers can give you as much or more information than the right ones. Many industrial products developed by accident. For example, Post-it notes developed at 3M as the result of a mistake. The glue was too weak, but someone saw the possibilities of paper that would stick, yet could easily be removed. So Post-its were born; they may have never seen the light of day if they had been seen as a failure rather than an opportunity.

○   Rewards can turn tasks into a means to an end. If you are promised a reward for completing a task, it makes sense to finish as quickly and expeditiously as possible. The task stands between you and the reward. You are likely to avoid the challenging parts of the tasks because there is a higher risk of failure. Rewards may thus discourage creativity, systemic thinking and the very challenges that need to be met.

CAN REWARDS DEMOTIVATE?

This question reminds us of a joke. An old man lived alone in a house on the outskirts of the village. He was tolerated as an eccentric. The local children enjoyed gathering at his gate every day, shouting insults and kicking the flowers in his garden. One day the man came out and met the children.

'You are not loud enough or rude enough,' he said. 'Tomorrow, I will give you all a pound if you come and shout the loudest and rudest insults you can think of.'

The children were delighted and the next day they arrived early and shouted long and raucously. The man emerged. 'Pretty good,' he beamed, 'Come tomorrow and do the same and I'll give you fifty pence each.'

The children thought this was still a good deal and duly turned out the next day to shout their insults. The old man came out again. 'Excellent!' he said. 'Come again tomorrow, but I can only afford to give you a penny.' 'Only a penny!' they shouted. 'No way!'

They never returned. The old man may have been eccentric but he was not stupid.

TEN WAYS TO DEMOTIVATE PEOPLE

It is much easier to demotivate people than it is to motivate them, just as there are more ways for your desk to be untidy than tidy. Here is a checklist of what *not to do*. As you read it through, ask yourself whether you have been using any of these behaviours. To demotivate people do any or all of these.

1   Ignore their achievements.
2   Assume you know what is important to them. Do not consult them, but if you do, ignore what they say, after promising to take it into account.

3   Take good results as the norm, but be extra sensitive and criticize any shortcomings.

4   Set standards that have no relevance to their work. Make many small rules and enforce them arbitrarily.

5   If they are not sure how to do a task, just tell them to get on with it. Don't let them bother you with their problems.

6   Be condescending, or failing that, sarcastic, especially in public.

7   Engineer situations where they develop a competitive fear of their colleagues.

8   Do not support them, but expect excellent results.

9   Take credit for their successes and blame them for failure.

10   Do not tolerate failure, and make people anxious to cover their tracks. This will ensure a climate of blame and distrust, and encourage political in-fighting that will interfere with work.

INTRINSIC MOTIVATION

So rewards do motivate people – to work for rewards. They buy behaviour not motivation. This would be acceptable if the behaviour was of good quality, but it is not guaranteed. The more creative the person the less their productivity can be geared to rewards. The human imagination can be rewarded, but not motivated by reward, just as you cannot motivate yourself to grow taller. Extrinsic rewards work against intrinsic motivation. When we talk of motivating people we want them to work well to bring their energy, personality, persistence and creativity to enrich the work they do. This type of energy comes from within. It is of course possible to move people to do something by threatening or rewarding them. The energy that 'moves' people, which is the basis of motivation, comes from within and from the individual values of that person. Motivation is no substitute for congruence.

Congruence is the feeling of wanting to work because it is intrinsically satisfying. You, as a manager, need to create the best conditions where people's interest can flourish, and remove the restraints that might stop them. This is no small achievement, and they will notice and appreciate your efforts.

Leadership is a much used and misused word in management. For us a leader is someone who creates intrinsic motivation, even in difficult conditions. Someone who inspires people to do things because they want to, rather than because they have to. Being a leader means treating people well and as far as possible fulfilling their values. Changing the way people are treated is likely to boost productivity more than changing the way they are paid. People do not have to be motivated from without to do a task that they find intrinsically interesting. It is not too great an exaggeration to say that much that goes under the name of motivational training is an attempt to patch over dissatisfaction about working conditions. It is to cover up the fact that some work is boring and repetitive and neither engages our emotions nor brings out our skills.

Equally, individual motivation is no substitute for organizational vision. It is at the wrong level. When many people are demotivated and dissatisfied they are simply demonstrating that the organization has lost its direction and vision. Try to change the organization, not whip up motivation. An organization that needs a lot of motivational training is in bad shape.

LEADERSHIP

Of a great leader, the people will say, 'We did it ourselves'. (Lao Tzu)

Leadership is another nominalization – an abstract word that hides a verb – leading, taking action. The word 'lead' comes from a root meaning 'path' or 'journey'. Leaders take people on a journey. Leadership has been in the forefront of management thinking since the end of the 1980s, and now nearly all managers are exhorted to be leaders as well. To manage is no longer enough, and this is hard to put into practice when managing seems quite demanding in its own right.

We believe the challenge for each manager is to evolve their own leadership style. In our experience this springs from a clear sense of self and knowing your own values and goals. Furthermore, the most successful leaders do not seek to create a dependent following. They assume that a leader's task is to help all his or her people to be leaders themselves.

Leaders empower; they give responsibility; they bring out the best in people, qualities they did not think they had. They create an environment to which people want to belong, where they can realize their potential. People are easily led in the direction that they themselves want to go. In that sense they are not being led passively, they are active participants.

On the individual level a leader inspires and intrinsically motivates people through their own values.

On an organizational level a leader is someone who can translate a vision into action through self and others.

The rapidly changing nature of business and the market has highlighted leadership skills. In times when change was slow and the market stable, an organization could survive and even prosper with a hierarchical administration, with leaders concentrated at the top. They set the vision, and sold it or told it to their people. This model worked in the 1960s and 1970s; large, stable, hierarchically organized firms dominated the market. Management could concentrate on maintaining the status quo. The 1980s were more turbulent, the decade of the entrepreneur. Small companies sprang up and became big companies based on the vision and flair of leaders – for example, Anita Roddick, Richard Branson, Alan Sugar. In the stormy seas of the 1990s times are changing faster still, the boat is constantly rocking, and management consultants like Tom Peters say we should capsize it ourselves regularly anyway and build another.

Leaders inspire change and provide a focus for individual loyalty. They embody the values that are important to the people they lead. All managers have leadership qualities insofar as they inspire and motivate their people by acknowledging and paying attention to the values that are important to them. 'Managers are people who do things right, and leaders do the right things' as the saying goes. Managing operates more on the logical levels of environment, behaviour and capability. Managing is making others do things. Leading is making others want to do things. Thus leaders operate on the values and identity for both people and the organization they work in.

We believe there are three main qualities of leadership: vision, trust and congruence, i.e. being a model of what you say – 'walking your talk'.

CULTURAL INFLUENCE ON LEADERSHIP

In Britain and the US, leadership is generally a positive attribute. We admire good leaders and tolerate poor ones. Not all countries share our assumptions. Several consultants were conducting a seminar on leadership in Moscow. The Russian business people at the seminar had an intensely negative response to the idea of the manager as leader. To them, leadership was associated with tyranny, corruption and brutality. They had to search back to Christ before they could identify an admirable leader.

The consultants paced and acknowledged this strong feeling without trying to change it. They then started to lead by opening the possibility of non-religious leaders with positive qualities. They did several exercises to reframe the idea of leadership as something that could be positive in practice, gathered more examples and experiences and started to unravel all the negative associations the seminar participants had to the idea of leadership.

VISION AND VALUES

Leaders embody a vision – a set of goals and values. As a leader you not only set a direction, but also move yourself and others in that direction. The first person you need to lead is yourself. Unless you believe in what you are doing – unless you are congruent – no one will join you. This vision does not have to be a great strategic revelation, but it must engage you for people to keep you company.

○   Firstly, as a leader, be clear about your own values and outcomes.
○   Secondly, you need a sense of the organizational vision.
○   Thirdly, you appeal to the values of the people you are leading.

A leader brings together personal, interpersonal and organizational values.

DISCOVERING WHAT IS IMPORTANT

Leaders motivate people by finding out what is important to them. They release intrinsic motivation. They elicit the values of the people they are with. A leader needs to know the values of everyone on the team. To elicit people's values ask questions like:

> What do you want?
> What is important to you about . . . ?
> What do you value about . . . ?
> What do you achieve by doing this?
> What matters to you here?

Questions beginning with 'why' will also establish values:

> Why is this important to you?
> Why do you want to do this?

You may not be used to asking such questions, and perhaps no one has ever asked you them either. The questions may seem somewhat personal. Remarkably, most people will be quick to tell you what is important to them and truly motivates them, if they trust you, and they will be delighted that you are taking the trouble to ask. You are paying them a compliment by asking, listening and pacing them by acknowledging their values. This may be the first time in their life anyone has asked. People often grow cynical and resigned in their work to not obtaining what they want. That you are interested at all is a step forward. Some people may be suspicious. They may expect they will have to justify logically what is important to them, or explain it in some way. If this happens, pace their suspicions by acknowledging them. Say you are genuinely interested and you will take whatever they say without asking them to justify it. Values are not logical.

Next you need to understand their rules – what has to happen for them to know that their values are being honoured? And, what has to happen for them to know that their values are being violated? What will they hear, see and feel? Ask questions like:

> How will you know that you are . . . (value)?
> What tells you that this value is being fulfilled?
> When did you last know that someone was honouring this value?
> What happened then?
> What did you see and hear and feel in that situation?

These values questions are probably the most important ones in this book. When you take the trouble to find out what is important to people you have the key to management and leadership.

Suppose a person says that in order to work well he needs to feel his job is challenging and worthwhile. You have the value, now you need the rules. Naturally, you ask, 'What lets you know that work is challenging and worthwhile?' You want specific behaviour. You may receive the answer, 'I get a feeling of being stretched. I know I am learning something new.' So you ask, 'And what would the company need to do to stretch you and for you to learn something new?' You will then start to obtain some specifics – a particular sort of work, some specific area, a form of training etc.

Now you can backtrack to check. Ask: 'And if the company did these things, then would you know the work was challenging and you were learning something new?' You want an emphatic 'Yes!' If you receive a hesitant 'Yes?' then you will have to continue by asking: 'What else would the company need to do?'

As people begin to talk about what is important to them, their physiology will change. They may become more animated, their face will change colour, their voice tone will change. Values may be expressed in abstract words, but they are far from abstract. They engage people at a deep level. You can see it in their faces and hear it in their voices.

THE SAGE ON THE STAGE OR THE GUIDE ON THE SIDE?

Leadership puts vision into action. Leaders inspire others. They have to be able to communicate the vision to others in a way the others understand. Leaders need communication skills. However, leadership is often confused with charisma, and the military connotations of the word 'leader' linger on in ideas of impassioned oratory, and the upturned, enraptured faces of the followers. Leaders do not need such a charismatic presence or indeed a high profile at all. Often they are most effective when they keep a low profile. A high profile attracts criticism and opposition simply because it is so visible; the message can become lost in the histrionics and the ceremony.

Leaders exert influence. It is important to remember that. They will have their own personal style of how they influence – that is secondary. The guide on the side can exert as much, or more influence than the sage on the stage.

The two greatest orators of their day in ancient Greece were Socrates and Demosthenes. When Socrates made a speech, the listeners would react by saying, 'What a great speech.'
When Demosthenes spoke, they would say, 'Let us march!'
Of the two, Demosthenes was the leader.

TRUST

Trust people and they will be true to you. Treat them greatly and they will show themselves great.' (Emerson)

Trust is the foundation of leadership. Trust in yourself, and the trust you show others and they show you. These three go together. By trusting yourself and others you are seen as trustworthy. Trust is built from pacing. First you pace yourself. You use your skills and strengths and are clear about your own values and goals. What you say aligns with what you do. The rapport skills discussed in Chapter 2 will also help you create trust with others. Trust is built when people see that you are a model of the vision you are offering. A vision of a great team working together as equals, where each contribution is equally valued will not catch light if the leader plays favourites, or makes unilateral decisions without consulting other team members, even if those decisions are good ones.

Trust is built by practising what you preach and by treating people as if they are trustworthy. A man who trusts nobody is apt to be a man that nobody trusts. In practice, this means that you act from a number of empowering presuppositions about yourself and others. We do not say these are true, but we know they are useful operating principles.

O   Everybody comes to work to do the best they can. You give them responsibility and create the conditions in which they will give their best. If you act as if the opposite is true, then you will be riding an endless carousel of rewards and punishments, and you will have to manage people's motivation. This is a heavy burden, one you can do without. When you help make a work place where people want to be, motivation is not something you have to create, it is natural. In that sense a leader does motivate people, but indirectly.

O   Everybody has all the resources they need, or can acquire them, therefore no-one is hopeless or helpless. Very often people have resources in another context, but forget, or think somehow they do not apply in a different environment. For example, we know one young man who can take car engines apart. He was able to bring the same skills of analysis, understanding complex structures and persistence to his first office job, once he realized he had them. Unfortunately, all too often talents go unused. Find out what people are good at and discover how they can use those qualities in their work. Make sure that no-one leaves their brains at the gate when they come to work.

O   Everyone acts with a positive intention. When you act as if this is true, you will look beyond behaviour to a person's beliefs and values. The behaviour may be difficult, ridiculous or even reprehensible, but you can honour the intention behind it. Work with that person to find other, more satisfying ways of meeting that intention.

O   The meaning of the communication is the response it elicits in the other person. You have probably experienced acting with a good intention only to find the other person responded negatively. You may have felt aggrieved and misunderstood. Your behaviour meant one thing to you and something else to the other person. Most people tend to cling to the idea that, 'the meaning of my behaviour is my positive intention'. However, when it is someone else's behaviour, they operate the opposite standard: 'The meaning of your behaviour is the response it elicits in me'. *As long as people operate this double standard they are going to be inconsistent and powerless.*

Once you take responsibility for your behaviour as the response it elicits in some one else, you gain power. It is not that their response is necessarily correct, it is simply their response and you have to deal with it whether you like it or not.

To be a leader you have to take responsibility for the results of what you say and do. You act on the four pillars of NLP that were outlined at the beginning of this book. You establish rapport and trust. You set a fixed outcome, purpose and vision. You notice feedback, the response you are getting to what you are doing. And finally you have the flexibility to change what you do in response to the feedback, to achieve what you want. Those four pillars are a blueprint for leadership.

We are not saying that these beliefs are true. We do not know. We do know that if you *act* as if they are true, and notice the results you achieve, you will be acting as a leader.

A LEADERSHIP MODEL

A leader must hold the balance between:

○   The needs of the individual. Good leaders develop the people they work with and bring out their leadership qualities. They pay attention to and respect their values.

○   The needs of the team. A leader aligns the team or group, not by papering over differences, but by encouraging differences and resolving them. The differences in thought and style and way of working enrich the team and make it more creative. The leader is always asking the question: 'How can these differences between people be used to work together more productively?' The best teams may have a nominal leader, but all members will have leadership qualities.

○   The needs of the task. The leader's responsibility is to ensure that the project is completed successfully. Leaders can achieve extraordinary results by making exceptional demands on themselves. Others in the team respond by matching. It is leadership by example. In any endeavour there is always a balance between task and relationship. When the task is clearly defined, the relationship between team members is relatively unimportant. When the task is not clearly defined or ambiguous, and people are unclear, then the relationship makes the difference between success and failure. Because leaders invest in relationship, they thrive in situations of uncertainty, change and ambiguity.

○   Their own needs. We do not support the vision of a workaholic leader who neglects his health and his wider community. An unresourceful leader is no good to anyone, and a workaholic is someone who confuses time put in with results achieved. A leader is part of the team, and so caring for the team means caring for one's self also. Some models of leadership tend to leave out this personal dimension, but the first person to lead is yourself. (See Figure 8.1.)

THE THREE TYPES OF INFLUENCE

There are three kinds of authority or influence that one person can exert over others. The first is positional. A manager has a position of authority and responsibility for his or her people, which is not dependent on personality or style. They may be a heartless autocrat, and provoke resentment at every turn. Whether people like them or hate them is irrelevant unless it interferes with their work or the work of their department.

The second kind of authority is related to knowledge. When you are an expert and have access to information, you exert authority within that defined sphere. Senior people will listen and do as they are told. Authority by virtue of skill or knowledge bypasses positional authority. A computer engineer may rank below a manager in the company structure, but when she tells you how to run a program, or you call her in because your computer is down, then you pay attention to what she says. Influence through knowledge is playing havoc with rigidly run hierarchical structures.

Lastly, there is influence by example. This is not dependent on the other two but enormously enhances both of them. It is also very powerful

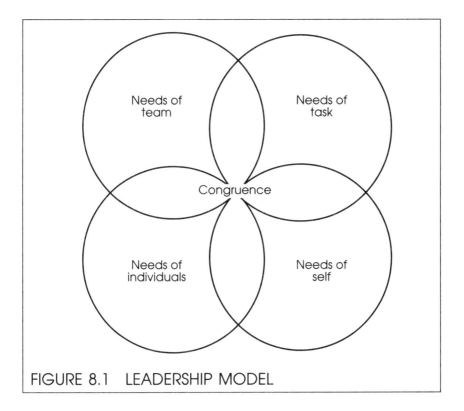

FIGURE 8.1   LEADERSHIP MODEL

on its own. It is the leader's greatest quality. Role models are usually more effective than control systems.

Although you will hear the phrase, 'Oh he / she is a born leader', we believe that leadership is not some mysterious inbuilt talent. Leaders are needed in times of change, and such times encourage leaders, but in every time there are people who have the ability to inspire others. We believe leadership is learnable. It is not an identity you are born with. NLP provides the how-tos of leadership – being clear about outcomes and values for yourself and others. Everything we have said in these chapters about outcomes and values is relevant to leadership. Leaders need the skills to communicate their vision, and NLP has a rich model of communication skills both verbal and non-verbal.

LEADERSHIP QUALITIES

A leader:

○   Builds a vision for self and others of an inspiring future in the long term.
○   Takes responsibility for communicating that vision to others.
○   Motivates self and others through shared vision and example.
○   Paces and acknowledges what is important to self and others.
○   Is a leader to him/herself.
○   Develops others as leaders.
○   Balances own needs with the needs of other individuals, the group, and the task.
○   Leads by example rather than knowledge or position.

THE LOGICAL LEVELS OF LEADERSHIP

There will have been times in your life when you were a leader – maybe at school, perhaps in further education, in sport, or in your family, perhaps with your children. Leadership is everywhere, it is not confined to the board room. When you inspire others and put vision into action you are acting as a leader wherever you are. Take a moment to think of such a time.

You already have the resources to be a leader

You may not have noticed, because it may have been in a context that you do not associate with 'leadership'. Or you may think that because you showed those qualities intermittently and for a short time span, somehow they do not count. You do not have to act like Napoleon twenty-four hours a day to qualify as a leader. With NLP all you need is a whisper of the quality for a short time and you can grow it substantially if you choose. It need only be a seed.

As soon as you recall an instance, however brief, of when you acted as a leader, ask yourself the following questions and write down your answers in as much detail as you want.

○ Think about your environment when you acted as a leader. What situation were you in? Who was there? What made it easy for you to lead there and then with those people?

○ What did you do? Think of the actual behaviour. What did you think? What actions did you carry out?

○ What skills did you use? Were there particular ways of thinking that you employed? Did you use any physical skills? How were you capable of being a leader?

○ What did you believe when you were a leader in that situation? What was true for you at that moment? What did you value? What was important to you then?

○ Who were you then? Who are you now? Are you different? If so, how? How do all the things you have discovered about being a leader fit into who you are?

MODELLING LEADERSHIP QUALITIES

Think of three leaders you know. They can be in any area of your life, not necessarily at work. They may even be fictional – from film, television or books.
What are their outstanding qualities?
Is there anything about their appearance that marks them out as a leader?
Is there anything about their voice that marks them out as a leader?
What skills do they possess?
What beliefs and values do they have?
What responses do they elicit from others?
Which of their qualities would you like to assume?
How does it feel to do this?
Can you now imagine yourself receiving the same sorts of responses from others?

DEVELOPING YOUR SKILLS

1   Take some time to find out the values of a work colleague. Make sure you have rapport. When you have established their values,

backtrack so that you are both sure. How do they respond to your interest in what is important to them?

2   Review your most important values and add your rules. What has to happen for each value to be fulfilled? What has to happen for each value to be violated? Notice if any of these rules are met in the course of a day.

3   Elicit a colleague's rules about their most important values.

4   Consider each of the four empowering presuppositions in this chapter:

O   Everybody comes to work to do the best they can.

O   Everybody has all the resources they need, or can acquire them.

O   Everyone acts with a positive intention.

O   The meaning of the communication is the response it elicits in the other person.

How would your experience of work change if you were to act as if they were true?

Pick one of the presuppositions each day. Then choose one interaction for that day and act as if your chosen presupposition were true in that situation for as long as you are comfortable doing so.

FURTHER READING

Adair, John, *Effective Leadership*, Gower 1983.

Bennis, Warren, *On Becoming a Leader*, Hutchinson Business Books 1990.

Harvey-Jones, Sir John, *Making it Happen*, HarperCollins 1988.

Maslow, A. H., *Motivation and Personality*, Harper 1954.

O'Connor, Joseph, and Prior, Robin, *Successful Selling With NLP – The Way Forward in the New Bazaar*, Thorsons 1995.

Peters, Tom, *The Tom Peters Seminar – Crazy times Call for Crazy Organisations*, Macmillan 1994.

NOTES

1   McGraw, Kenneth, 'The detrimental effects of reward on performance', in M. Lepper and D. Greene (eds) *The Hidden Costs of Rewards*, Earlbaum 1978.

2   Deutsch, Morton, *Distributive Justice. A Social–Psychological Perspective*, Yale University Press 1985.

3   Kohn, Alfie, *Punished by Rewards*, Houghton Mifflin 1993.

4   Deming, Dr W., *Out of the Crisis*, Cambridge University Press 1988.

9

BUILDING A COMMON LANGUAGE

❖

Organizations are created by people. Their intention is to make it easier to come together for a common purpose. The structure of an organization must serve the needs of the people who work in it. They are, after all, its greatest asset. Good managing comes down to obtaining the best from yourself and your people – creating structures and using the structures that are there in order to do so. One of our greatest resources is our imagination. The unwritten subtitle of this book is 'managing the human imagination'.

CLOSING THE CIRCLE

One of the most fascinating areas of NLP is the interplay between organization and individual – how individual ideas, hopes and fears are expressed in an organization, and how organizational purpose and vision takes on a life of its own, greater than the sum of its parts. We began this book from an individual perspective: rapport skills and pacing and leading. We moved on to organizational vision and mission and the mutual effects on individual values and outcomes. Now we will close the circle by returning again to individuals.

This chapter examines how to create a common language for understanding and being sensitive to the way people are thinking and feeling. It will give you a refined awareness of body language and behaviour and an ability to influence people in your organization. Understanding and obtaining the best from your people is a skill that is often taken for granted, and is hard to measure. Often it is left to the manager's 'intuition' or 'natural talent'. NLP takes such talents and models them into learnable skills. 'The age of communication' frequently refers to the technology rather than the social skills to use and explain the technology. New systems and information technology will not yield its maximum benefits without good interpersonal communication skills.

VICIOUS AND VIRTUOUS CIRCLES

What happens when you communicate? You use your body language, words and voice tone. They listen, make sense of what you say in their mind, think about it and reply. You listen, think and answer in turn. What each of you says is influenced by what you have just heard. Conversation is an ebb and flow (see Figure 9.1).

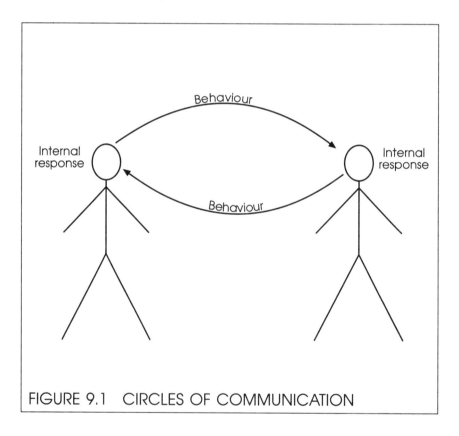

FIGURE 9.1   CIRCLES OF COMMUNICATION

These circles can be vicious or virtuous. They can lead deeper into misunderstanding and conflict, or into agreement and understanding. We are sure you can think of many examples of each in your day-to-day work. Rapport and second position help to keep these circles virtuous rather than vicious. The other person's different understanding keeps the circle moving. They think differently, so the meaning they give to our communication is going to be subtly (or not so subtly!) different from the one we intend. So how do we make meaning of what is said to us?

HOW TO BUILD AND DEMOLISH A MEMORY

Think of a recent work meeting. Close your eyes if this makes it any easier. Think back to what the room looked like, and the faces of the people who were there. Hear their voices again as best you can, and any other sounds that may have been in the room. Think back to how you felt. Was the chair comfortable? Was coffee served? Did you smell it? Can you remember what the taste was like? What did you feel emotionally at the meeting? Did it go well?

Now blank out all the pictures of the environment and the people present. Next, silence all the voices and sounds in your memory. Now lose all the smells, tastes and feelings. Is there anything left? You may still be talking to yourself, but that is about the meeting, not the actual meeting itself. When you stop that voice, what is left of the meeting? You had the initial experience through your senses. You recreated the experience through your senses. They are your experience on the inside. NLP proposes that a useful way to think about thinking is using our senses internally.

THINKING ABOUT THINKING

All our experiences, whether triggered internally in our imagination or externally in the environment, come through our senses. When you think of your boss, you are likely to 'see' a remembered image. (How else do you recognize him or her when next you meet?) We do not have the world in our head, but a representation of it. What we see and hear is selective, depending on our interests, preoccupations and state of health. We remember only a small selection of what we notice for the same reasons. For example, you are unlikely to remember the colour of every colleague's tie from yesterday, because it is not important, even though they were right in front of you.

We are also selective in our feelings. You are not likely to be aware of the feeling in your left hand until we mentioned it. It is just as important to forget as to remember, otherwise we would be constantly overloaded. We are not 'objective' observers, or tape recorders. If we were, we would all agree on everything, whereas the only thing that people have in common is that they are all different.

We react to our selective representations of the world, not the world itself. There are some tremendous implications to this. Change your representations and you can change your reaction. Change your patchwork pattern and the world changes. We have an extraordinary ability to create experience on the inside that has real effects on the body. It is impossible to say where 'mere' thinking ends and body experience begins. Nothing is 'all in the mind'. Think of a painful memory and you will wince again. Thinking of a good memory will bring back the good feelings. Imagine eating your favourite food and you will salivate. On a more serious level, continued stress has been shown to contribute to stomach ulcers and heart disease. Our thoughts have powerful effects on us, regardless of what we do about them. How we represent what we see, hear and feel is very important. We use our senses on the inside to 're-present' what we have sensed on the outside, so in NLP the senses are called representational systems.

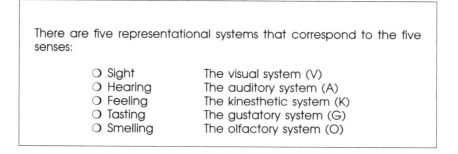

There are five representational systems that correspond to the five senses:

○ Sight	The visual system (V)
○ Hearing	The auditory system (A)
○ Feeling	The kinesthetic system (K)
○ Tasting	The gustatory system (G)
○ Smelling	The olfactory system (O)

The visual system can contain remembered images (what you had for breakfast), or constructed images (the CEO with green hair). The auditory system can contain remembered sounds or voices as well as constructed ones (the sound of a piano bouncing down the stairs). The kinesthetic system has several components: feelings of balance, touch from the outside world, and emotions. We make meaning of our sensations through our values, beliefs, interests and preoccupations. Emotions are our feeling responses to these meanings that we make of our experience. They do not arise out of thin air, they are triggered by how we have represented our experience internally.

THINKING AT WORK

We all have preferences about how we think. Just as some people have a sharp eye, a keen ear, or feel strongly, so we develop certain ways of thinking more strongly than others. If you have a visual preference you may be interested in the visual arts, television, films, mathematics or physics. It is difficult, for example, to be a good graphic designer without the ability to imagine detailed, vivid pictures that you can translate onto the paper. With an auditory preference you may be interested in training, language, writing, drama or music. With a kinesthetic preference you may be interested in athletics, sport or dance. We use all these different ways of thinking, just as we use all our senses, but some we use more than others, and they will be more developed.

Learning styles are one immediate application of representational systems. For maximum impact learners need to see, hear and experience what they are learning. They need to see – visual displays, graphs and diagrams; they need to hear – lectures, talks and tapes; and they need to experience – role plays, practice and rehearsal. When you train someone at work, use all the senses. However, different people also have different strategies for learning. A strategy is the consistent order in which they use the representational systems to think. For example, one person may want to see the material first, then talk it over and then feel how it fits together. Another may want to hear about it, then see it before making a plan. You need to pace different strategies, those of your boss as well as those of your co-workers. This is also important in sales – pace the customer's preferred way of taking in information.

IF IT IS NOT IN WRITING, THEN IT'S NOT REAL

John discovered that his boss needed to see written reports. John was more auditory and for a long time used to talk over his work and then wonder why his boss didn't pay much attention. 'Why does she want it in writing?' he complained. 'I've already told her all about it twice!' Because she had a visual preference. If it wasn't in writing it wasn't real to her. Once he paced her by writing a summary, she was open to talking about it, which satisfied him as well.

When you know how people think, you can understand what is important to them and what annoys them. People who think in pictures often find it difficult to work in an untidy environment, it distracts them. They will want to keep their workplace neat. People who think in sounds are easily disturbed by noise. Perhaps you have heard someone say, 'Be quiet, I can't hear myself think!' Other people need to be comfortable – a different chair can make a big difference to how well they work. By knowing these preferences you can arrange your own environment in the way that suits you best and respect the needs of others.

DOING WHAT WE THINK

Our brains are not isolated from the rest of our body, how we think is reflected in our body language. Look at the cartoons. Who's angry? Who's bewildered? Who's deep in thought?

Cartoonists working on paper, television or film have to draw feelings and states of mind, and they do it by making the body language obvious. Certain gestures and postures often go with emotional states. We intuitively understand them. Here is some of the body language that goes with the

different ways of thinking. While not immediately apparent, it becomes obvious once you pay attention. When people visualize they tend to look up, or level, perhaps staring into the distance. They may furrow their brow as if trying to focus on something, as indeed they are (their internal pictures). When someone does this while you are talking to them, it is usually best to stop talking. They are inside their own head and not paying attention to you. When 'visualizing' people will also tend to stand or sit erect and breathe high in the chest. Their breathing is shallow, so they tend to speak quite quickly. Pictures can change fast, and it is possible to see a great deal of information in a picture all at once. Visual people also need to see who they are talking to; when on the telephone, they will usually create a mental picture of the caller. They feel uncomfortable if the person they are talking to face to face is not looking at them. For them, this is equivalent to not listening. The kinesthetic, however, may want to look down while listening to feel comfortable, which can lead to loss of rapport on both sides.

When thinking in pictures people tend to:

○   Look up, defocus or stare into the distance.
○   Breathe high in the chest.
○   Sit or stand erect.
○   Talk quickly.

The body language that goes with auditory thinking is different. People make small rhythmic body movements or sway from side to side. They will often have a pleasant, musical voice. They may put their head to one side as if they are listening to something and indeed they are. You may see their lips move as they talk to themselves.

When thinking in sounds people tend to:

○   Put their head to one side as if listening.
○   Breathe in the middle of the chest.
○   Use their voice expressively.
○   Move rhythmically.

Kinesthetic thinkers think with their body. They often have a slumped posture with rounded shoulders. They tend to breathe slowly, from the abdomen, and they talk more slowly and in a lower pitched tone. A conversation between a kinesthetic and a visual thinker can be a frustrating experience for both parties, as the visual thinker drums their fingers with impatience at the slow delivery of the kinesthetic, and the kinesthetic does not follow the breathless delivery of the visual thinker. These are general patterns, not stereotypes.

When thinking in feelings people tend to:

- ○   Look down.
- ○   Breathe low in the chest.
- ○   Have a relaxed posture with rounded shoulders.
- ○   Talk slowly.
- ○   Talk in a low pitched voice.

Watch people's eye movements. Have you ever wondered whether they mean anything? Eyes do not flop around at random in their sockets. NLP suggests there is a connection between eye movements and the way we think. In NLP they are known as eye accessing cues because by making them we 'tune' our bodies to make it easier to access certain ways of thinking.

Here are the general patterns that hold for most right-handed people. People tend to look upwards or defocus when they visualize – usually up to the right for constructed pictures, to the left for remembered imagery. Their eyes move to the side when they are hearing sounds internally, and they look down to the right when they are thinking in feelings. They look down to the left when they are talking to themselves. This is known as internal dialogue. See Figure 9.2.

Cartoons show general, stylized body language that is immediately understandable. However, the principle only applies so far. Most body language is on a much subtler level and is not so easily predictable. Every individual is unique. We cannot assume that the body language we manifest ourselves can be extended to the rest of the world. For example, we may frown when disagreeing; a visual person may frown when concentrating, because they are tightening their facial muscles trying to see things more clearly on their mental screen. Do not make the same mistake made by one

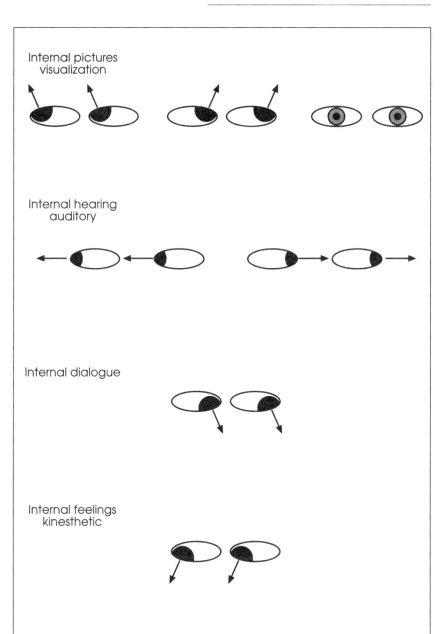

Internal pictures
visualization

Internal hearing
auditory

Internal dialogue

Internal feelings
kinesthetic

FIGURE 9.2   EYE ACCESSING CUES (General patterns
for right-handed people, from onlooker's viewpoint)

British police force. When first told of eye accessing cues, they assumed that if the suspect's eyes moved up to the right before answering a question, they were lying, because that movement is generally associated with constructed rather than remembered mental imagery. There are at least two mistakes here. Firstly, some right-handed people and most left-handed people move their eyes up right to remember pictures. Secondly, because a picture is constructed does not make it untrue.

You can, however, recognize certain movements and postures of *one particular person*. This is called *calibration* in NLP. Calibration is recognizing another person's internal state by reading their body language. As you begin to observe these minimal cues that everyone is showing all the time, you will begin to see some patterns emerging. The cues are not random, certain responses occur repeatedly in certain situations. At times the individual will say what the response is by describing how they feel. For example, a colleague frowns and says, 'I can't work this out.' You infer that he is puzzled. On another occasion you notice the same expression and he is silent. You might ask, 'Are you having difficulty working that out?' and he responds with a 'Yes.' Another time when he frowns, you might say, 'It can be hard to work out.' Your colleague is likely to feel that you understand his experience.

When you recognize these subtle signs you will be able to see the effect of what you say on the people you talk to without guessing or mind reading. As the saying goes, 'Leadership is the ability to alter the second half of your sentence based on the response you receive to the first half.' But first you have to see the effect of the first half.

Your organization may do market research to find out what your customers want and will monitor figures from within the organization to track staff and production processes. NLP takes this to the individual level by detailing how you can understand your colleagues and customers. We use these ideas a great deal in our sales training. Customers will signal their willingness to buy, or their objections, in their body language before they verbalize it, indeed they may not verbalize it at all. The good salesperson sees the resistance and adopts another approach. The unobservant salesperson stumbles on down the blind alley.

In our culture it is no exaggeration to say we are trained not to notice other people's responses at this fine level. And if we do notice them, we learn not to attach any significance to them. We pay a great deal of attention to the words spoken and not much conscious attention to how they are said. Even the spoken words hold more information than appears at first hearing.

WORDS OF WISDOM

NLP takes language as a literal expression of our inner experience. Consider three people who have just attended a presentation. The first says: 'That was very *enlightening*. I can *see* how this strategy will *focus* us on the key issues. We can *examine* the present situation and foresee *difficulties* ahead.'

The second person says: 'That was an excellent *discussion*. The main points came over *loud and clear*. We have to *ask* ourselves these sorts of questions before we can *tell* what is going to happen in the next decade.'

The third says: 'The main points came over very *strongly*. Unless we can *get a grip on* our corporate strategy and be *sensitive* to market changes we are going to find ourselves *out in the cold* before we can *catch our breath*.'

These are three possible ways to refer to the same meeting. The first person uses *visual* words, the second *auditory* words, and the third *kinesthetic* words. They are extreme examples to make the point that language reflects our thoughts and therefore the representational system we use. These sensory-based words are known as predicates in NLP. Here are some common examples; you can see how they sound to get a feel for the idea:

Visual words and phrases
Look, visualize, reflect, clarify, reveal, outlook, foresee, vision
The future looks bright
A flash of inspiration
Shed some light on the matter
An illuminating remark
I see what you mean
Looking closely at the idea

Auditory words and phrases
Say, sound, tell, discuss, listen, ask, talk, demand
Talking it over
In a manner of speaking
Tell it to the Marines
Turn a deaf ear
Ring the changes
That message comes over loud and clear

Kinesthetic words and phrases
Touch, solid, rough, grasp, gentle, hold, sensitive, hot
I will be in touch with you
A firm foundation
Hold on for a second

Let me grasp the point
Too hot to handle
I can't put my finger on the fault

There are literally thousands of these sorts of phrases, some we say without thinking ('I see what you mean'). There are also olfactory and gustatory phrases (He smelled a rat, a nose for business, the sweet smell of success, a taste for danger, left a bad taste in the mouth). And some people even talk about 'eating your words'.

Here are some common phrases 'translated' into different representational systems:

Neutral	Visual	Auditory	Kinesthetic
consider the idea	look at it	sound it out	get a grip on it
I understand	I see	I hear what you say	I feel I get it
I don't agree	We don't see eye to eye	We are not on the same wavelength	Our ideas clash

Many words do not have a sensory base, such as know, recognize, decide, think, learn, motivate, change, consider. When you pay attention to the way different people talk you will probably discover that most people have a preferred way of expressing themselves, which reflects their preferred representational system.

MATCHING THE LANGUAGE

Matching predicates is a powerful way to establish rapport. When you match predicates you are literally speaking the other person's language. For example:

Visual: I'd like to *see* you so that I can *show* you what I have in mind and we could have a *look* at how it might *appear* in future publicity.

Response: I *see*. A meeting certainly *looks* like a good idea. I'll have a *look* in my diary and *see* when we consider your proposal. Thursday *looks* good.

Auditory: I just *called* to *ask* if we could fix a time to *discuss* things. I want to *have a word* with you about what I have in mind so that we can *talk through* how it might be used in future publicity.

Response: I *hear what you're saying*. A meeting certainly *sounds* like a good idea. I *tell* you what, what about Thursday, then we can *talk through* your proposal.

Kinesthetic: I *feel* it would be useful *to touch* base so that we can *get to grips* with what I have in mind and *get a feel* for how we could use it in future publicity.

Response: I *like* that. A meeting certainly *feels* like a good idea. I'll find a time in my diary when we can *get to grips* with your proposal and *toss it around*. Thursday is clear.

PACING THE LANGUAGE

Here are some statements. Choose a response that paces the sensory words:

1 I don't see how this idea will work
    (a) Let me give you another perspective.
    (b) Let's try and crack the problem.
    (c) It's hard to grasp, I'll run through it again.
    (d) What exactly don't you understand?

2 I can't get anywhere in my discussion with the project manager.
    (a) I'll see if I can help you make an impression.
    (b) How can we get you two on the same wavelength?
    (c) He always struck me as hard to handle.

3 I can't get a grip on this project costing.
    (a) Let's talk it over.
    (b) I'm not comfortable with it either, let's turn it over together.
    (c) Let me see – looks like a lot of work here.

These are straightforward examples for you to start matching other people's language.
Answers: 1(a), 2(b), 3(b)

A person who has been using mainly visual predicates will probably understand clearly given diagrams and pictures. It will be clear to him what needs to be done because you are showing him. A long and detailed verbal description would be far less effective. He may quite literally not be able to see the point of what you are saying.

The same holds true organizationally. A few years ago a colleague of ours was hired by a leading manufacturer of luxury cars to research the selling strategies of outstanding salespersons and to create a programme to teach these strategies to other salespeople. Success meant that he would be running the training – a lucrative contract. He did his homework very thoroughly. Yet even as he was in the midst of the training he had that sinking feeling that it was not going well, and delegates' feedback confirmed his feeling was right. Yet every participant recognized that the material was valuable. It became company policy for every salesperson nationwide to attend the training during the following eighteen months. But our colleague gained absolutely no benefit because he had been commissioned to design the programme and it was now the motor manufacturer's property. While they were very happy with the programme they were unhappy with his style of presentation, so they always used their own trainers.

When he asked them specifically what he should have done differently to have won the training contract they were hard put to answer. They talked of the training room looking 'untidy'; of how he had failed to turn off the overhead projector when changing slides which made the presentation 'messy'; and of how delegates were not used to what they called a 'cluttered' training manual. Eventually one of the company's trainers summed it up: 'It just did not have the right look for our sort of company. Looks are very important to us.' He had made the mistake of thinking that the content of his work would be sufficient. His presentation failed to pace the corporate culture, which placed great value on the visual. What were minor details to him were organizational rules of that visual culture. They could not see eye to eye with him.

COLOURFUL, TELLING, IMPACTFUL LANGUAGE

The more you use sensory language the more you engage the senses, and the more vividly you communicate. The more vivid, the more interesting – and the more interesting, the more memorable. Why do so many presentations seem boring? Because they are given in non-sensory, or 'digital', language. Any experience can be drained of life with bloodless language.

Listen to this passage from an 'action' training: 'These pulleys will be attached to these ropes which will, in turn, be attached to these trees. On completion of the construction of the Tyro lean Traverse, as per the technical directions given by Nigel and myself, which are within the specification of the brief. The person going number one on the Sierra south side will be attached to the two aforementioned pulleys, and with the assistance from the November North side, will make a longitudinal movement along the catenary . . .'

Believe it or not, this was the trainer's introduction to a team exercise that involved crossing a ravine. The initial excitement of the trainees disappeared in the first minute.

There is an art to holding another person's attention. To engage it you have to paint a picture that makes the experience come alive – it is the art of the storyteller, the after-dinner speaker and the professional writer. Back in 1962 the doyen of public speaking, Dale Carnegie, observed:

> In the process of getting and holding attention, the first purpose of the speaker, there is one aid, one technique, that is of the highest importance. Yet it is all but ignored. The average speaker does not seem to be aware of its existence . . . I refer to the process of using words to create pictures. The speaker who is easy to listen to is the one who sets images floating before your eyes. The one who employs foggy, commonplace, colourless symbols sets the audience to nodding . . .'[1]

With NLP we can take this further. It is not only pictures that are important, it is equally vital to engage our other senses. You do this by using a mixture of predicates. This is important when speaking to a group. Let the visual people see what you mean, give the auditory people something to listen to, and the kinesthetics something they can grasp. By addressing their main channel you will gain a person's attention. Saying it in other ways may be repetitious but, if anything, that is an advantage – communication research suggests that repetition is important if you want your message to be remembered. Saying the same thing three times in different ways will ensure that if your audience does not understand the message the first time they will probably pick it up on one of the subsequent laps. And this is true whether your audience is one or a thousand.

HOW TO GIVE AN ENGAGING PRESENTATION

- ○ Vary your voice expressively.
- ○ Speak in active sentences with a subject, verb and object (e.g. 'X did Y', rather than, 'Y was done').
- ○ Give your audience your full attention.
- ○ Use sensory language – colourful, telling and impactful.
- ○ Provide adequate breaks, at least every hour.
- ○ Use visual aids such as slides or videos.
- ○ Use interactive exercises to make people stand up and move about.

HOW TO GIVE A BORING PRESENTATION

○   Use little variation in voice tone.
○   Speak in passive sentences with an impersonal subject (e.g. 'It was done' rather than, 'Someone did it').
○   Do not look at the audience and pay them very little attention.
○   Read from a prepared script.
○   Use lots of nominalizations (abstract nouns).
○   Continue for well over an hour before your first break.
○   Keep still.
○   Do not use slides or videos and keep visual input to a minimum. (You will notice that the ceiling or floor suddenly becomes fascinating to a large number of listeners.)
○   Do not have any interactive exercise which would make people move about.

WHY ARE SO MANY COMPANY DOCUMENTS BORING?

Digital documents are hard to read. How would you like to read several pages in this style? 'With regard to the decision of the previous meeting relating to option five, insufficient data has been collected to determine whether a favourable resolution of the outstanding debt situation can be effected.'

There is a strange belief in management that the more abstract the language and the harder to understand, the more credible and important the document. Objectivity and professionalism have somehow become equated with abstract language. Now abstract language can be very useful when it refers to something of substance. Too often in business there is plenty of abstraction but nothing definite. In our example above, nothing specific has been said at all.

NLP has made a detailed study of the effects of language, and we can authoritatively say that this example is the language you would use to induce trance. We guess this was not the intention of the writer!

HOW TO WRITE AN EYE-CATCHING DOCUMENT

○   Use sensory words and phrases.
○   Write in active sentences with a subject, verb and object.
○   Use short sentences.
○   Lay out the document in short paragraphs and use a typeface that is easy to read.

○   Use relevant headings.
○   Use simple English rather than Latin-based words.
○   Give specific details where appropriate.

HOW TO WRITE A BORING DOCUMENT

○   Use many nominalizations (abstract nouns) and avoid sensory words and phrases.
○   Use passive sentences with an impersonal subject (e.g. 'It was done' rather than, 'Someone will do it').
○   Use long sentences with numerous subclauses, the result of which, if strictly adhered to, will be the gradual diminishing of interest in and understanding of the meaning of the sentence, however important it might be, and the subsequent amnesia for any pertinent point, if indeed any pertinent point was ever there in the first place, contained in it. (Do you cognize our meaning?)
○   Format the document in long paragraphs and use a small, difficult to read type.
○   Do not break up the document with any helpful headings.
○   Do not use a simple English word if two or more Latin-based words will do.
○   Avoid giving specific details.

The latter language is often found in jargon or insiders' vocabulary. Abbreviations and acronyms abound. One company, for example, issues its employees with a glossary of terms. Here they learn that an OAP is not an old age pensioner, but an 'Outside Awareness Panel' (otherwise known as a window). This language is often the enemy of clear thinking, specific targeting and decisive action.

Someone who habitually uses such expressions gives the impression of being aloof. If you want to achieve rapport with them, start by pacing. Match their language style. You will be able to establish some rapport and then lead them into some sensory-based conversation. Take your cue from their eye accessing cues. What the words don't say, the eyes will show. The person will still be using their senses on the inside. If they look up use visual language: 'You will see . . .'. If they look down to the right then: 'As you think about this, you may feel . . .'.

NEGOTIATION AND MEDIATION

Ian was called in as a consultant by the MD of a plastics manufacturing company. Two of his directors kept tripping each other up and the MD was at a loss to know how to proceed. Each was superb in his department and both were vital to the company's continuing success, yet if they continued clashing the company would suffer.

The only time available for Ian to meet them was half an hour in the departure lounge at Heathrow on the day they were both due to fly out to represent the company at an important exhibition. At the meeting, Ian soon found out that Jeff thought Bill was 'out of touch'. Bill thought Jeff was 'shortsighted'. From these simple statements it was clear that they had no understanding of what the other needed. Ian's job was very simple, it was to be a translator.

When Jeff remarked that he didn't feel right about Bill's proposal for company expansion, Ian would translate and tell Bill that it was as if Jeff's pictures were dark and jagged. This astonished Bill. He immediately saw that, if that's what the picture looked like, it wasn't surprising that Jeff was not supporting his proposals. Bill was no less enthusiastic about his vision, but he now recognized the need to describe it in more step-by-step detail. This slowing down was an important way of establishing rapport with Jeff who was much more kinesthetic. By the time their flight was called they understood what was happening between them and had arrived at a working arrangement for this business trip. Jeff would be responsible for the public presentations that were scheduled, while Bill would concentrate on building new client relationships by meeting people face to face.

It proved to be a very successful strategy. They came back rather pleased with themselves, having secured a large amount of business. Most striking was that they could not sing each other's praises highly enough. The MD was both delighted and puzzled. They had experienced how effective they were when working as a team.

Effective managing often means resolving differences to move forward. Being fluent with different language styles can transform working relations by making one person's way of doing things comprehensible to another who does things very differently. Different language styles point to different thinking styles and so different strengths. For instance, people who use mainly visual language and frequently adopt a visual physiology clearly have potential in looking ahead and dealing with charts, diagrams and plans. People who use mainly auditory language and adopt an auditory physiology may be good in discussions, good at listing the pros and cons, and good on the 'phone. Finally, people who use kinesthetic language and adopt a kinesthetic physiology will tend to foster relationships in the workplace, because they'll want colleagues to feel good about each other. This is worth remembering if you are team building. Every organization needs all three styles.

Going to extremes will look, sound and feel unbalanced. Ian once worked for a corporation that regarded the appearance of its furniture showrooms as supremely important. They sold expensive furniture and wanted it to look superb. As a consequence the showrooms were spotless. However, visiting them made him, and others, feel distinctly uncomfortable. It all seemed just too impersonal. A customer survey later reported that the showrooms were seen as clinical. People did not feel inclined to come in 'on spec'. They were slightly intimidated. It was like coming into an immaculate house and being afraid you will tread dust into the new deep pile carpet and offend your host. However, conveying this message required great diplomacy. It was as if the company's visual preoccupation had become part of its identity.

A visual, auditory or kinesthetic preference is one example of people's different thinking and working styles. The next chapter will explore some others that are just as important.

DEVELOPING YOUR SKILLS

Start these exercises in low-risk situations, e.g. at home with your family, or when you are with friends. When you become confident, you may want to try them at work.

1   Learn to become aware of people's body language. Does it support the words, or does it seem to give another message? A good place to start is watching people on television.

2   Notice the sensory words used by others in low-risk situations. Does anyone you know have a preferred way of expressing themselves? Again, start with people on television or radio. The more abstract the topic being dealt with, the more abstract – and therefore the less sensory specific – the language will probably be.

3   Discover your own representational system preferences. Write a brief description of your day at work (or dictate it to a tape recorder if you prefer). Do it quickly, using the first words that come to you. Look at or listen to it afterwards and count the number of predicates in each representational system. The one with the most is likely to be your preferred system. Do this on three different occasions.

4   In order to match the individual style of your colleagues and customers you will need to be fluent in all three systems (visual, auditory and kinesthetic). Practise by writing memos in the three different ways. Then write the same memo with a mixture of words. Do it purely for your own learning until you feel confident.

If you carry out these four activities with some consistency you will find that your awareness of people's predicates will develop very rapidly. When you decide to use these new skills in your work, it will probably be easier than you think. Many managers have told us that, far from having to pay close attention to determine a person's language style, it became glaringly obvious to them after a while.

FURTHER READING

O'Connor, Joseph, and McDermott, Ian, *Principles of NLP*, Thorsons 1996.
O'Connor, Joseph, and Seymour, John, *Training With NLP*, Thorsons 1994.

NOTE

1   Carnegie, Dale, *Effective Speaking*, Association Press 1962.

10
WORKING STYLES

❖

W e pay attention to different parts of our experience, filtering all we see, hear and feel through a screen of current interests, pre-occupations, beliefs and mood. The ability to selectively ignore and forget is just as important as the ability to notice and remember, or we would drown in information. We habitually notice some experiences and screen out others which results in consistent patterns in the way we think and work. This chapter helps us to understand some of these working patterns – NLP calls them metaprograms – and consequently to understand the strengths and weaknesses of our own and other people's working styles. Metaprograms are a huge area. We will summarize some of the important ones and point out the main applications and implications for management. Some metaprograms may be familiar. Some of these patterns you may find bizarre. Others you will sympathize with – they are likely to be your own.

TAKING THE INITIATIVE

There was an interesting study at Bell laboratories reported in the *Harvard Business Review*. Researchers analysed differences between average and top performers – in essence an NLP modelling project, but without the NLP distinctions. Both types of performers said they regularly 'took the initiative'. How the different groups understood 'taking the initiative' was interesting. The average performer said that it meant dealing with information, for example, writing a memo to a supervisor about a software bug. The stars, however, said that taking the initiative meant fixing the bug yourself. The same word, 'initiative', had two very different interpretations, one to do with reacting, the other acting.

'Taking the initiative' for the top performers – doing something directly – is being *proactive* in NLP. Its complement, being *reactive*, means a tendency to bide your time and rely on others to deal with the issue. Proactive people act, reactive people react. Most people are a mixture of proactivity and reactivity. Being proactive is generally encouraged, and empowerment enables people to be more proactive. However, people can only be as proactive as the company structure allows them to be. It is useless to hire proactive people in a reactive company culture. No one will have a chance to be proactive in a company that lurches from crisis to crisis forcing its people to react to short-term emergencies.

WARNING!

Warning 1

We are not making value judgements on any of the patterns we write about. They are equal and complement each other. Outwardly it seems as if proactivity is always good and reactivity not, but this is not so. It depends on what sort of work you are doing.

Warning 2

These patterns do not define people by type or put them into neatly labelled boxes. They describe behaviour, not people. They are also tendencies not absolutes, for example, no one is all proactive or all reactive.

Warning 3

Like values, metaprogram patterns will change depending on the context. A person may be proactive at work, reactive at home.

Warning 4

Although some people may show these patterns in an extreme form, most show a mixture of the two.

PROACTIVE / REACTIVE

Proactive people initiate action. They are 'self starters' and work well on projects that they initiate. They may make mistakes by judging issues too quickly without gathering enough prior information.

Reactive people wait for others. They want to understand the situation before acting. They are good at analysing tasks and gathering information prior to acting. They respond to others. They may hold up work by too much initial analysis. Indeed they may assume that the only possibilities are those dictated by circumstances.

CARROTS AND STICKS AGAIN

How do you maintain your concentration on your work? Some people think about goals. They move *towards* what they want. Others want to avoid loss. They notice difficulties and want to solve problems in advance. This is called *away from*. A towards pattern is generally encouraged in business, especially in outcome setting. Towards people believe in the carrot as motivation, away from people believe in the stick – motivation by avoiding trouble.

Towards people are often attracted to the selling profession, with its traditional system of monthly sales charts, rewards and incentives. If you are in sales, recruit towards sales people. Pace and respect those of your people that tend to be away from. They are invaluable for pointing out dangers and problems in advance. The way to influence away from people is to point out the danger in not taking action; they will already have seen the dangers in taking it. Financial services and insurance companies employ many away from people who do excellent work pinpointing risks.

Do you have colleagues who constantly sail close to the wind with deadlines? Who seem to need a looming deadline to tackle the task? They are probably away from. The unpleasant consequences of not finishing drives them to finish (sometimes). When they do not have deadlines, they lack incentive and may not finish.

TOWARDS / AWAY FROM

A *towards* person moves towards goals. They set out to achieve, and concentrate on their goals. They are best managed by giving them work that is goal oriented. They may not be good at anticipating problems or finding errors.

An *away from* person notices problems, difficulties and situations to be avoided. They often use the pressure of deadlines as an incentive to finishing their work. They are best suited to work that entails finding errors – auditing, quality control and software 'debugging'.

WHAT DO WE DO ON MONDAY MORNING?

A direct marketing agency we know was pitching for a large contract with a client firm. Although they put their proposal together with the utmost care, it was unsuccessful. They were disappointed. However, they had an opportunity to debrief their clients. They asked what they had done wrong. The clients said that the basic proposal was good. They could understand the concepts. But then they said: 'We couldn't foresee what we would be doing on Monday morning.' At which point anyone who has studied metaprograms would say, 'Aha, the proposal was too general.'

People who are comfortable working in a comprehensive framework, the global view, have what is called a *general* metaprogram in NLP. They are happiest looking at large chunks; they concentrate more on the outcome rather than 'how' it is done in sequenced steps. This is the area of strategic planning and setting directions, the mission and vision of the company.

Equally important, although in a different way, is the person who is concerned with *detail*. They take the large plan and chunk it down into a sequence of small, achievable steps. They build the big picture like a jigsaw puzzle. Detail people are good at chunking down, they will examine the whole plan and tell you exactly what you will be doing on Monday morning. The direct marketing agency needed a detail person on their team to balance their proposal.

GENERAL / DETAIL

A *general* person is good with large chunks of information. They consider the framework of the task as a whole and are good at strategic planning. They may talk in generalities, and are more interested in total concepts than sequences, steps and stages.

A *detail* person is most comfortable dealing with small chunks of information. They work well with details and sequences. They may use many modifying adjectives and qualifications when they talk or write because they try to make the statement as precise as possible.

ADVERTISING THE DIFFERENCE

One of our friends acted as a consultant to a fast growing advertising agency, generally considered as pioneers in the field. They have a reputation for producing work that is innovative and different from previous campaigns. Anna gave us a fascinating insight into how they work. She was present at a briefing given by the creative director when they had acquired a new client. He posed his creative team three questions:

> 'What is the business reality at the moment for our client?'
> 'What are the current rules of advertising for this business area / product?'
> 'How can we break all of these rules?'

Here is a man driven by finding what is different. He wants to know the rules so he can break them. In NLP this is known as a *mismatching* metaprogram, or sorting by difference. We all make comparisons. Some of us, like the creative director, concentrate on differences. They look to break rules. Beware of giving such people routine work, they will look for ways to vary it; they thrive on work that constantly changes. If it does not, they may change jobs. They also look for exceptions to the rule. Every team needs at least one mismatcher. They will point out new directions.

Mismatching is not quite the same as finding the counter example. Some people are very good at finding where proposals do not work, and the downside of any plan. Both mismatching and finding the counter example seek balance, and are both different from polarity responding. A 'polarity responder' is driven to contradict what you say. This is often a way of asserting their identity. Their favourite phrase is 'Yes, but . . .', which can be wearing. Pace polarity responders by letting them know you value their expertise in finding exceptions; utilize their skill when you need it. If you want to avoid an argument with them, phrase what you say in the negative. Rather than: 'This is what we will do', say something like: 'I am not sure if this is what we will do'. Being very consistent, they will now mismatch your negative and uncertainty and begin arguing in favour. For readers who polarity respond, this section may not be exactly what you were looking for . . .

Mismatching helps to build innovative business. Anita Roddick, founder of the Body Shop, puts her corporate philosophy as follows: 'First you have to have fun. Second you have to put love where your labour is. Third you have to go in the opposite direction to everyone else.'[1] Masura Ibuka, the co-founder of Sony says: 'The key to success for Sony, and to everything in business, science and technology . . . is never to follow the others.'[2]

The complementary pattern is *matching*, or sorting by similarity. People who match notice what stays the same about people and events. They are often comfortable doing the same work, and may change jobs infrequently. Some people notice similarity first and then the exceptions; they usually like changes to occur gradually and slowly and like their work to evolve over time. Other people notice differences first then similarities.

Imagine a conversation between a general, proactive matcher and a detail, reactive mismatcher – it's a combination made in Hell. The proactive matcher will be looking to move forward to achieve the goal, and being general, will be thinking about the overall plan. The reactive mismatcher will see all the dangers and pitfalls, and worse still, will pick over the details. They could easily drive each other crazy. If you are in the invidious position of having these people on your team, pace and lead them. Appreciate the point of view of each; they are truly complementary. Your end result will be a detailed plan with minimal risk to achieve a specific goal, and with a well thought out high-level concept.

MATCH / MISMATCH

People who *match* look for similarities, they are good at generalizing from a few examples and will look for areas of mutual agreement. They are usually good at mediation. They may be satisfied doing a task for some time before wanting to move on.

A person who *mismatches* looks for difference. They are the rule breakers, often innovative, but may shun the standard procedure for no other reason than it is standard. They will be good at tasks that change and evolve quickly, or as members of a team that is constantly doing different work.

HOW EASILY ARE YOU CONVINCED?

Imagine you have a new person on your team and have given them a task to do. How would you convince yourself that they were competent?

○   Would they need to do it a number of times for you to be convinced? If so, how many times?
○   Would you give them the benefit of the doubt immediately and assume they are competent?
○   Would you need to see them in action over a period of time before being convinced? If so, how long would that period have to be?
○   Are you never completely convinced? Do people have to consistently prove themselves competent? Whatever happens today, could it be different tomorrow?

Many managers are convinced either by a number of times, or a period of time, depending on the complexity of the task. A few give the benefit of the doubt from the start, noticing only evidence of incompetence after that (sorting for difference). A boss who wants consistent evidence is the hardest to work for. This pattern also influences how people regard their own competence at a task. Some need to do it a number of times, some for a period of time, some assume they can do it, and for others every time is like the first.

What sort of evidence do you need? Some people need to see the evidence; they want to see the person working, or see the work they have done. Others need to hear the evidence. They will ask colleagues. Some people need to read reports and references. Lastly (and this is rare with managers) some need to work alongside the person before becoming convinced (or not) that they are competent.

BEING CONVINCED

There are four ways in which a person might seek evidence either that they, or others, are competent at a task:

O   They need a number of instances.
O   They need evidence over a period of time.
O   They don't need convincing – they give the benefit of the doubt.
O   They are never really convinced – every time is new.

The evidence may need to come from a particular source:

O   Some people need to see the evidence.
O   Some people need to read about it.
O   Some people need to be told.
O   Some people need to do it.

FOLLOWING PROCEDURES

The next pattern is very important in management. Some people are good at following *procedures*. They follow the set sequence. They enjoy doing the task the 'correct' way and may be at a loss if they encounter difficulties. Other people want *options* – to have choices and develop alternatives. They hesitate to follow well-worn procedural paths, although they are good at developing them. Even when they develop the procedures, they are unlikely to follow them. They like to develop alternatives. In sales, you will find it hard to make an options person follow a script. When you want alternatives to established ways of working, options people will supply them.

Both patterns are important. At certain stages of business you will need to develop procedures. Procedures simplify and automate complex tasks, making learning easier. Accountants need to be procedural, so do filing clerks. Many areas require clear procedures and in this instance you want compliance rather than creativity. Beware of recruiting options people if you then give them strongly procedural work.

PROCEDURES / OPTIONS

Procedures people are most comfortable following established procedures that give them a definite task sequence.

Options people will seek to vary any set procedure once they know it. They are good at developing procedures and alternatives.

LOOKING INSIDE OR OUTSIDE

How do you know when you have done a good piece of work? There are two types of answer. The first is something on the lines of: 'I just know'. People who reply like this are strongly *internal*. They have their own standards and use them to decide what to do and how to judge their success. Strongly internal people will insist on deciding for themselves and will resist the decisions of others on their behalf. Adopt a very light touch when managing people who are very internally referenced. They are often labelled as 'stubborn' and need minimum supervision.

The second type of answer is: 'When other people say so'. People who reply like this refer to the outside for confirmation. This is called *external* reference. Externally referenced people expect others to set standards. Such people need a management style with much praise and guidance. They need constant feedback or they become unsure. An internally referenced manager may lose rapport with her external people by not giving them enough praise and acknowledgement, thinking they do not need it – after all she doesn't, so why should they? An internally directed manager often takes a more paternal role and has a more direct leadership style. An externally oriented manager will be more concerned about harmony and consensus. Most people have a mixture of internal standards and also seek external feedback.

INTERNAL / EXTERNAL

An *internal* person wants to decide for themselves. They have their own standards. They may have difficulty accepting praise, and work best with little or no supervision.

An *external* person expects others to set standards. They need to be managed and want feedback on how they are performing. They do best when closely supervised and given clear feedback with examples of success.

USING THE PATTERNS

We have given a very short summary of some main metaprogram patterns, concentrating on the ones most useful in management. They are not meant to be explanations; they are patterns you may already have noticed. Most people show a bias towards one side or the other. What are the applications and implications?

KNOW YOUR OWN PATTERNS

The danger is managing others in the way you would like to be managed. By knowing your own patterns you can manage people in the way that works best for them. You will be pacing their reality. They will respond and work better. You will also be able to arrange your own work towards your natural strengths.

CONSIDER OTHER PEOPLE'S METAPROGRAMS

You will be more responsive to how your people work best and how to influence them if you have first found out about other people's metaprograms. You will also be able to allocate work to the natural strengths of your people, or give them challenges when appropriate. If you do the latter, pace them by telling them it is a challenge as well as a task. Understanding metaprograms makes delegation easier.

You will start to see beyond surface disagreements between team members. All metaprograms are useful in some situation; they balance each other. Some arguments are futile: whether a glass of water is half full or half empty. Who is right? Both. The matcher will say it is half full, the mismatcher will say it is half empty. (The polarity responder will try to find a way to prove them both wrong.) In particular, understand the metaprograms of your immediate boss, so you will know how best to present ideas to him or her. Find out your boss's preferences and priorities.

Metaprograms provide a powerful way of understanding behaviour and resolving difference. What looks like a policy dispute on the surface often turns on personal issues between managers. In one company where Ian was consulting, directors were constantly disagreeing. Two were hardly on speaking terms. The company reflected this conflict. There was much internal politicking, hidden agendas and personal bias. Part of Ian's work involved interviewing everybody at senior level and eliciting their metaprograms. It turned out that the senior director was very towards, general and options oriented; he loathed following procedures. He was internally referenced and mismatched the rest of the management team. Three other key staff, including the head of administration and finance, were very procedural and dealt in detail. The more flexible managers who might have been able to translate between them were too junior to have a significant effect. All the people concerned had passionately good intentions.

MATCH JOB TO PATTERN

The proactive person will initiate action. They are likely to be good at outside sales, new project management and active networking. A reactive person might be more at home in work that requires input, for example a sales clerk or a bank teller. External people are good at being adaptable to customer needs. Proof checking is ideally suited to someone who mismatches at a detailed level (looking for small mistakes).

BUILD YOUR TEAMS FROM A MIXTURE OF PATTERNS

Value the input of all the team members. A team made up of general, proactive, self-referenced matchers will work together famously, but may not produce anything that can be used. (The ideas will be great though.)

CONSIDER THE METAPROGRAMS OF YOUR ORGANIZATION

Organizational metaprograms are interesting. What patterns are encouraged in your company? Which patterns does the company structure reinforce and which does it inhibit? Management programmes imply certain metaprograms. For example, many organizations maintain quality by inspection. This is a mismatch; you are looking for those products that are not up to specifications. TQM thinks about this differently. It aims to control the process variability so that you achieve the same result every time. That's a match.

Some managers have an incongruent culture. They encourage their people to be towards and aim for goals, while making it clear by example that mistakes are not tolerated. People are motivated to avoid mistakes because the consequences are unpleasant, and this contributes to an away from culture. To add insult to injury they then complain that their people are not sufficiently motivated to achieve goals.

Your organization may be very internally referenced, in which case you may fail to learn from other organizations. For example, Xerox learned from a worldwide mail order sportswear shop that was picking up orders three times faster than they were. Rather than looking internally and aiming to improve by a percentage of your own current performance, look outside to industry standards. You may need to make basic changes in order to keep up with your competitors. Different departments may have different metaprograms – indeed they should have. People with an options mismatching metaprogram are likely to be at home in research and development. The accounts department needs a good share of procedural, detail people.

TIME TO ACT

Now for time – that most important commodity. There never seems enough of it. Work expands to overfill the time available for its completion. A great deal of time is maintenance – simply keeping your department on the level. Then there are the crises that have to be dealt with. Between all these calls are those small chunks of time that are your own, the oases in the desert, when you can carry on with work you need to complete. The problem is that this discretionary time comes in small pieces, sandwiched between the routine and the imperative, hardly ever in a large enough chunk to allow you to accomplish very much.

There are libraries of books on time management, and we do not intend to take up much time with the subject. NLP has one highly significant contribution to make in this area. Time management schemes assume that we all experience time in the same way. We do not. Time is a subjective experience and that is the realm of NLP. The trouble with many time management schemes is that they suit people who think in the same way as the designer of the scheme, and these are precisely the people who do not need the scheme.

We measure time externally by distance and motion – a moving hand on a clock face. How do we think of time internally? We must have some way of representing time in our minds, otherwise we would not be able to tell if a thought is a memory or a plan for the future. How do we know? How do we represent it in our minds?

HOW DO YOU EXPERIENCE TIME?

Think for a moment of something you saw and heard that happened yesterday. Now think of something that happened last week. Now think of something that happened about a year ago.

From which direction do these memories seem to come? If you were to intuitively point to the direction, where would it be? To the left or right? In front or behind you?

Now think of an event that you anticipate in the future. From which direction does that seem to come?

When you have established where your past memories seem to come from as well as your future hopes, notice how they are connected by a line. This is your *timeline* (see Figure 10.1).

Most people use space and direction to represent time mentally. For some people the past seems to come from their lefthand side. The further to the left the more it is in the 'distant past'. The future goes off to their right, and the further away the 'further off' in the future it is. The point of 'now' will usually be right in front of them. In NLP this is known as a timeline that is 'through time'.

The other type of timeline is known as 'in time'. Here the past is behind you, the future is in front of you, and you experience 'now' inside you, you are in the timeline. There has been a great deal of research on timelines in NLP, for the way we organize time in our minds has profound implications for the way we manage our lives. We will confine ourselves here to some of the practical business implications.

Time management schemes are for the most part designed by through time people for through time people. Planning is much easier for people with a through timeline: the past, present and future is laid out in front of them and it is easy to see the connection between what has happened, what needs to be done now, and what should happen in the future. A through timeline is important for long-term planning. People who are through time find it easy to establish and stick to deadlines and they expect others to do so too. Through time is the prevalent timeline in the Western business world: 'time is money'.

People who are in time concentrate more in the present moment. Because of this they tend to be less good at planning, setting deadlines and ordering and sequencing their tasks. If you do not have this type of timeline imagine what it would be like if you never spread out a wall calendar to look ahead, but always had it rolled up so that you saw only what was happening today. In time people may seem less dependable and interpret

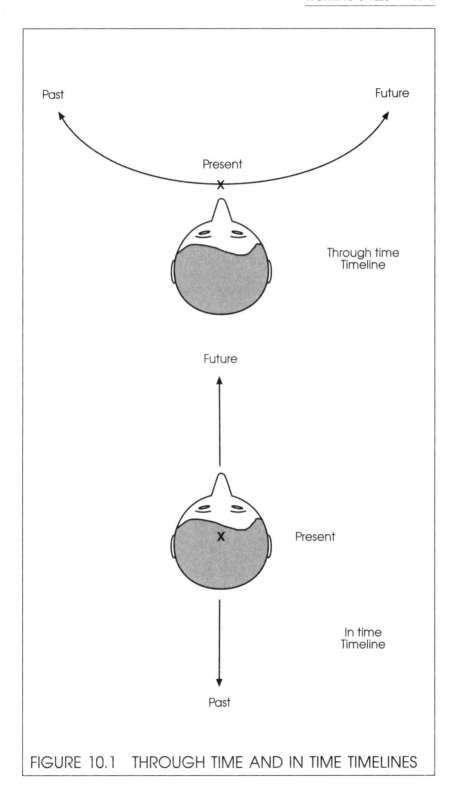

FIGURE 10.1   THROUGH TIME AND IN TIME TIMELINES

deadlines and appointments more flexibly. They do not lack energy or skill, they simply do not connect what they are doing now with what will happen in the future. They are the sort of people who will look at their diary and say in astonishment, 'How on earth did it get so full?'

There are three underlying skills to good time management:
- ○   Set your outcomes and think them through carefully.
- ○   Prioritize your outcomes.
- ○   Plan your time from a through timeline.

PLANNING THROUGH TIME

Both kinds of timeline are useful, neither is inherently superior. It depends what you want to do. You do not need to change your usual timeline. However, if you are planning make sure you do it from a through time perspective.

Imagine a timeline laid out in front of you from left to right like a year planner. It is usually easiest to have the past on your left and the future on your right, as this accords with the usual eye accessing cues (eyes left for remembered images and sounds, and right for constructed images and sounds). It may be easier to do this on the floor using pieces of paper for the various tasks and arranging them in sequence in front of you. Make a written plan of tasks with deadlines and map them onto the timeline in front of you. Work across a sheet of paper from left to right rather than starting at the top and moving down. Whenever you look at the plan imagine it in front of you. Notice what has been done, what needs to be done and whereabouts you are in the complete task.

Finally, what sort of timeline does your organization have? How far does it see itself stretching into the future? Is it so intent on dealing with problems now that it is failing to plan for the future? How far does it stretch into the past, and is that history available to learn from? There is always time ahead, but do we see a future in it for ourselves?

MODELLING EXCELLENCE IN BUSINESS

The patterns we have considered contribute to how easy people find their work and how well they do it. Some people are very good at what they do;

others do not have the same flair. NLP is built on modelling – finding out how exceptionally able people work, so as to teach it to others. NLP business modelling can be used in two ways:

O   Build a profile of the exceptional people in your organization, and hire others based on that profile.

O   Model the top performers in the business area you are interested in, for example, sales, project managing, negotiation, interviewing, or coaching.

An NLP modeller will discover the mental strategies used by the top performers, the beliefs and values as well as metaprogram patterns. A training course can then be designed to teach these patterns to others who need them, as well as to new recruits. (If you are interested in arranging a modelling project see the consultancy section on p. 194 of this book.) Modelling can be used for very specific skills and also very general areas. For example the NLP trainer and developer Robert Dilts has carried out an important research project using modelling to identify the skills of leadership for a leading Italian multinational company. NLP can make the skills of the best more widely available. Even a small increase in individual skill can make a big difference to the effectiveness of an organization.

DEVELOPING YOUR SKILLS

1   Look at the habitual ways you sort information. What metaprogram patterns do you favour at work? Where do they work well?

2   Notice situations which tend consistently to cause you a problem. What metaprogram patterns are you using to resolve the situation? Might another pattern be more useful?

3   Consider other people's metaprograms. Notice their habitual patterns and, where appropriate, offer information in the way they prefer.

4   When you delegate, what metaprogram pattern would be most useful for completing that task? If possible, find someone who shows that pattern in their work.

5   Think about the metaprograms of your organization. One useful way is to look at its advertising. What metaprograms does the advertising appeal to?

FURTHER READING

Charvet, Shelle Rose, *Words That Change Minds*, Kendall/Hunt 1995.
Dilts, Robert, *Skills for the Future*, Meta Publications 1993.

James, Tad, *Timeline Therapy and the basis of personality*, Meta Publications 1988.

Kelley, Robert, and Kaplan, Janet, 'How Bell labs creates star performers', *Harvard Business Review*, July 1993.

O'Connor, Joseph, and McDermott, Ian, *Principles of NLP*, Thorsons 1996.

O'Connor, Joseph, and Prior, Robin, *Successful Selling With NLP*, Thorsons 1995.

NOTES

1   Roddick, Anita, and Miller, Russell, *Body and Soul*, Ebury Press 1991.
2   Schlender, Brenton, 'How Sony keeps the magic going', *Fortune*, June 1993.

11
FINALE

'Gain power by accepting reality.'

Chinese proverb

This chapter will bring together the threads of the previous chapters by concentrating on you and your relationship with the organization. You need to influence many people to deliver results, and the last two chapters have been about how diverse people are: how they pay attention to different things, how they have different values and different ways of thinking. We have argued that the best way to influence is to be a leader, and to make leaders of those below you. People's expectations of their work are different. Organizational change has changed the art of management in a fundamental way. And management is an art, it is concerned with how to extract the best from yourself and others, to harness the power of the human imagination.

Money will usually solve the hard issues. That leaves the soft issues for you to deal with – relationship, motivation, and eliciting the best from people. Your skills in these areas will amplify your results. By handling people well, you will achieve more from them and yourself than you thought possible. Handled badly, they will amplify any discontents and problems.

Managers have to balance and allocate scarce resources – money, skills, equipment, training, and particularly time. Demand always seems greater than supply. Management theory is about planning and co-ordination; in practice we know it is not so simple. Daily routine and disruptions conspire to break the tidy picture. When Henry Mintzberg carried out his stopwatch survey in 1989[1] on how managers passed their time, he found they spent an average of nine minutes on each task before being interrupted.

A successful manager needs not only to be able to manage the status quo, but also to initiate and deal with change. Hierarchical structures and functional departments are changing in favour of networks and goal-focused teams. No one is indispensable. In this age of redundancy and re-engineering, management is more insecure than in the past. NLP can supply some of the essential tools a manager needs to survive and prosper now, and for the future.

LOOSE CHANGE

Change rarely goes smoothly. Organizations are complex systems and the procedures and structures that make them effective also resist change. People will resist change if they fear it, or see no reason for it. Many organizational change programmes falter because they leave people in the dark and do not communicate the rationale behind the change. Therefore in any changes you make, involve the people who are affected. Tell them what is happening. Above all, *make sure you know the positive by-products of the existing structure and incorporate them into the changes you make.*

FOUR IMPORTANT BELIEFS FOR *INEFFECTIVE* CHANGE MANAGEMENT

○   Changes must start at the top.
○   Managers act and lead, employees react and follow.
○   Managers push and argue, employees resist and object.
○   Managers listen to objections in order to marshal better arguments to overcome them.

FIVE IMPORTANT BELIEFS FOR *EFFECTIVE* CHANGE MANAGEMENT

○   Changes can begin anywhere.
○   The leaders of the changes may not be obvious, but may come from any level of the organization.
○   People will co-operate if they have good reason to do so.

O	There are good elements to the present situation that need to be incorporated into the change.
O	Pace objections before leading – the objections contain important information about the present situation that can be used.

Most people do not believe it is easy to make substantial and permanent changes in their own or others' basic characteristics or style. Managers often spend time simply trying to make people see that there is a problem at all. The more you know of your people's 'default mode' – that is, their basic metaprograms, preferred representational systems, favourite perceptual positions and values – the more easily you will be able to inspire their best work. You will not need to change their basic way of working. The more they know of NLP, the more they themselves will be able to utilize their strengths.

When you want someone to change their behaviour, tell them clearly what you want. Do not hope for instant transformation, but agree between you a way of monitoring the change over time. Be clear about the logical level you are operating on. Beliefs and values are very resilient. Unless you are highly skilled, or NLP trained, you are unlikely to effect them in the short term. A change in capability needs time and training. Do not ask for a change in capability unless you provide the means to achieve it. Most change will be on the level of behaviour. Give the person the responsibility for the change. Value them for what they are. Confirm the person's identity and values and be clear you are asking for a change in behaviour. Individuals strongly oppose change if they perceive you are asking them to change values, beliefs, or identity.

I'VE WORKED HARD TO REACH WHERE I AM – WHERE AM I?

NLP is a valuable tool for managers, and you do not have to give anything up to use it. NLP is designed above all to be useful. If it works use it. If you cannot make it work, use something else. Most of the tools are simple and very effective: pacing and leading, logical levels, and perceptual positions. A skilled craftworker may have very few tools in his toolbox but they are the best, and he can do more with them than others who have a toolbox twice the size. The tools are only as good as the worker, and any management system is only as good as the managers who use it.

Whatever the tool, you must both want to and be able to use it. This brings us to the area of emotional state: your moods and feelings. Some days you are full of energy, you feel you can accomplish miracles; other days it is an effort to start work at all. You have a responsibility to yourself as well as to others. In all the work you do with others in the organization, it is easy to forget that you are an important part of that organization, and if you do not feel well, then you will not work well. NLP is the study of the structure of subjective experience. It explores emotional states, how we get into them, what choices we have in them, and how we can change them. When you are in a good state, work is easy, the skills you know come easily and it is easy to learn. When your state is not good, work seems hard, and it is more difficult to deal resourcefully with others. The outside world has not changed, but your state makes it seem different.

Constant interruption and work pressure can affect your state. You may feel unresourceful, or 'stressed'. Stress comes from a clash between what we expect and feel confident we can deal with, and what the world throws at us. Environments do not produce stress of themselves. A person's interpretation of what happens to them is what causes stress, because we react emotionally to the meaning we make of events, not the events themselves. That is why two people can have totally different responses to the same event. Our internal model of the world sets up our expectations. The more flexible our model, the more perspectives we have, the better tools we have for dealing with work, the less likely clashes are to occur, and the more confident we will feel dealing with clashes. Stress is greatest when we think we have no control over what is happening. Thus the more you try to control the situation and fail, the more stress you are likely to experience.

There is only one part of the situation you have control over – yourself. By changing your reaction you can change other people's reactions and influence events. Control is perhaps the wrong word. It implies a rather mechanistic approach and you are not a machine. Choice is a better word. With NLP you can increase your choices about how you feel and how you react, and therefore how influential you are in any situation. You can also spare yourself a possible executive ulcer.

ANCHORS

Your states are constantly changing as you react to the environment. To have choice about your states, you need to know what triggers them. The sight and sound of certain things will change your state, for example, seeing a photograph, entering your office, hearing the fire alarm, a special piece of music, a plate of your favourite food, the smell of coffee. NLP calls any stimulus that changes our state an *anchor.* Anchors may be visual: the sight of your desk, or holiday photographs. They may be auditory: an advertising jingle, the sound of a colleague's voice; or kinesthetic, a handshake. They can be external, in the environment, or internal, within your mind. And they operate at every logical level, for example, your name is an anchor for your identity. Advertising seeks to link a particular image or sound to a product through repetition and make it an anchor for a desirable state such as relaxation, sexual attractiveness or freedom.

Anchors are universal and very useful, because of our ability to link a stimulus to a response. Society provides many anchors, and we make our own because we do not want to have to stop and think about everything that happens. You do not have to decide whether to stop for a red traffic light every time you see one. You just stop. Many anchors are neutral, and some trigger unresourceful states. We consciously choose very few of our anchors; they accumulate at random as we live.

MENTAL MANAGEMENT

There are two main practical uses of anchors:

O   Design your own anchors for the resourceful emotional states you want.

O   Notice those that put you in an unresourceful state. Once you know them, you can choose your response rather than simply react.

Have there been times when you wanted to remember a good idea yet you have forgotten it a few days later? If you want to remember, design an anchor for it. Every time you look at the anchor it will remind you. For example, a manager we know has a number of pictures and photographs on the wall of his office. He deliberately hung one upside down to remind him to take different perspectives on any issue besides the obvious one. Another has a small globe of the world on his desk to remind him that everyone has different models of the world.

A wall calendar can be an anchor to remind you to plan from a through time timeline rather than an in time timeline. A friend has a picture of the Tardis on her desk: the time travel machine of Doctor Who to remind her to plan through time.

For many executives, a family photograph on their desk top, is an anchor for a good state. You can use visual anchors, pictures, a vase of flowers, photographs, the view from your window (if it is one that makes you feel good). You can use auditory anchors such as a favourite piece of music. You do not even need external anchors. We all have the capacity to create good feelings and change our state by thinking of people or events. You can remember a good time in your life and in doing so recapture some of the good feelings associated with it.

CHANGING YOUR EMOTIONAL STATE

Think of a particular good experience you have had. It does not matter how long ago it was, or whether it was in your professional or personal life. Relive this experience now, seeing the people and things around you just as you did at the time. Hear the sounds again – the voices and other noises that were there, and enjoy again the good feelings associated with that experience.

The event is in the past, but the memory is in the present. You can recall these memories now in any way you like. You might like to experiment with your mental picture – make it bigger and/or brighter, and see if that makes the feelings more intense. Make the sounds louder and clearer and notice if that adds to your experience. You have just changed your emotional state from your own resources. You can do this any time you wish.

Memory is not like a scrapbook full of pressed dead flowers. The events live on. By reliving them, we can relive the feelings too – for good or ill.

BUILDING A RESOURCEFUL STATE

The key to using past experiences to gain resources in the present is to associate into them. You are associated when you relive the experience seeing it through your own eyes. The opposite of association is dissociation: when you see yourself in the experience, you are outside it, seeing it at one remove. A dissociated state is when you are thinking *about* things, not engaged in them. Dissociation is important when you are planning.

Dissociation is also useful for learning from past experiences. When you remember such experiences, instead of seeing them through your own eyes (associated), mentally step to one side and see yourself in that situation, acting in the way that you did. Dissociation keeps any unpleasant feelings at bay. Then ask yourself, 'What do I want in that situation?' When you know how you would have liked the experience to turn out, ask yourself: 'What would I do differently in that experience now, with the benefit of hindsight?' When you have decided what you would have done differently, associate into that new mental image and imagine yourself doing it.

Does it feel right? If it does not, dissociate again, and imagine a better response. Then step into that and imagine doing it. Dissociate when you are thinking of new responses, and associate when you mentally visualize the new response to 'see how it feels'.

When you have decided on a new response that feels right, mentally rehearse it in an associated way. Thus it becomes more memorable, more real and immediate, and more likely that, when a similar situation comes up in the future, you will *do it*. In NLP this is called *future pacing*: mentally rehearsing what you want to happen so you are already prepared when the situation arises. It is the basis of mental training in sports. You do have some measure of control over the pictures, sounds and feelings in your mind. In some ways it is easier to manage your inner world than your outer one.

ASSOCIATED AND DISSOCIATED MEMORIES

Think of a pleasant experience, and remember it. Be associated in the memory. See the event again through your own eyes. Notice the feelings you have.

Now think about the experience again, and this time dissociate. See yourself in that experience, doing whatever you were doing. Notice the feelings you have.

Which gives you the stronger feelings? Finish by repeating whichever gives you the strongest feeling.

WHAT SORT OF ANCHOR ARE YOU?

What states do you elicit in others? How do your superiors and subordinates feel when they see you? What do they expect? Are you a good news or a bad news anchor? Anchors build by repetition. If you constantly bring bad news, or are always critical, you become an anchor for bad states in other people. People avoid bad anchors.

How can you be a positive anchor for your boss and the people you manage, so they feel good when you are around? There are two ways:

○   States are contagious, so when you are in a resourceful state, you are more likely to be a good anchor for others. People want to be with other people who make them feel good; they may not know why, but they feel the attraction.

○   The second way is direct. Find out what they have done right and praise them for it. Tell them exactly and specifically what they did right. Praise, like criticism, has to be specific if it is to have any effect. When you praise, you will be a pleasure to work with.

ASSOCIATED AND DISSOCIATED WORK

Association and dissociation apply at the organizational level too. Most people are associated, engaged in their work, even if they are not enjoying it at the time. People who are dissociated from their work are 'not with it'. They will say things like: 'I'm just going through the motions' or 'I can't 'see myself in this job in a year's time'. Any organization with significant numbers of dissociated people is almost certainly in trouble – it is not engaging its people. They are not achieving what they want from their work. Their energy and creativity is likely to be going on something else.

---

10 WAYS TO SUPPRESS ORGANIZATIONAL DEVELOPMENT

1   Regard any idea from below with suspicion and insist that people go through several layers of managers to win approval.
2   Give contradictory messages.
3   Express criticism freely and withhold praise.
4   Treat problems as a sign of failure and blame individuals.
5   Demand results, set impossible deadlines, institute sanctions and punish mistakes.
6   Try to control every aspect of what people do.
7   Make decisions to change and reorganize in secret, and surprise people.
8   Control information and make people justify their requests.
9   Have short-term and long-term goals clash with each other.
10   Have many written rules and stick to them rigidly.

How many of these apply to your organization? To your boss? To yourself?

ANTIDOTES

A sense of curiosity
A love of fun
An ability to turn failure into feedback
A passion for experimenting
A taste for ambiguity
A belief in the enterprise of people

CONGRUENCE AND ETHICS

Does your influence derive solely from your organizational view and what you do? If it does then doing the job would mean everything else would follow easily. How you are perceived by others is crucial. Your greatest influence comes from who you are, not what you do. Congruence is the inner strength that comes from your sense of self. A strong sense of self comes from knowing your values and acting on them. It comes from knowing what you want, your strengths and potentials, and pacing yourself when necessary. When you are congruent your words and actions match up. You do as you say. Your body language reinforces your message. Congruence inspires rapport and trust.

Organizational congruence surfaces into the public view as business ethics. There is a growing debate about how business is to respond to issues such as environmental pollution, public safety, anti-discriminatory practice, and the rights and feelings of minorities. From the point of view of enlightened self-interest, companies need to forecast social changes in the same way they forecast changes in their own markets. Business is one of the greatest influences on society; it shapes social values and expectations, as well as reflecting them. This means that business needs to be ready to disclose, willing to be open to social views in return. Any failure by business to keep in touch with social responsibilities leads to society imposing rules and regulations with all their attendant difficulties and penalties. Where there is no trust, rules abound. This applies to the people within a company, as well as the company's relationship to the wider society. A company's vision statement cannot stop at the company doors – it must reflect and take into account the wider community. It is not just for the employees.

Ethical business means that the organizational vision is connected to a sense of the wider community.

Ethics has everything to do with management. Individual character flaws do not explain corporate mismanagement. There is usually a structure that allows misconduct to happen. When it does, the individual concerned may take some of the blame, but inevitably the ramifications go far and wide into the company, often leading to resignations at a higher management level and changes in company structure. The collapse of Barings Bank in 1995 is a perfect example.

THE PRICE OF ETHICS – 60 MILLION DOLLARS

In 1992 Sears, Roebuck & Company received complaints in over forty American states about its automotive service business. It was accused of misleading customers and selling them unnecessary parts and service. Management did not, of course, set out to cheat the customer. Management directives contributed to problematic sales practice. At the time, Sears' market share of the automotive service business was shrinking, and management tried to increase it by introducing goals and incentives for employees. Increased minimum work quotas were laid down, with product specific sales quotas, paying commission based on sales. Employees who did not meet these quotas would be transferred or have their work hours reduced. This put pressure on employees, who had little guidance about how to distinguish between unnecessary and necessary maintenance. There was little active management support for ethical practice to detect questionable sales methods. They did not appreciate the systemic effect of incentives, or foresee the wider consequences. No one seemed to go to second position with the automotive engineers to understand how they might react to this situation.

To their credit, Sears responded directly to the complaints by acknowledging management responsibility and stopping the practice of sales quotas for specific parts. They denied intent to deceive customers. The whole affair was very expensive for Sears – the total costs of settlements including customer refunds was about 60 million dollars.

Johnson and Johnson withdrew Tylenol capsules nationwide after some were tampered with – a reflection of their corporate vision, not simply a top management decision. Without a shared ethically sound vision, the company's response could not have been so swift and effective.

Congruence is also expressed through alignment with the company's vision. Management shapes and expresses the company's guiding values, to create an environment that supports ethics, integrity and a shared accountability among employees. A clash between a manager's individual values and corporate values is very uncomfortable; he or she needs to be congruent to pass on the organizational vision to others. Organizational ethics is a responsibility of management.

Congruence is not compliance. Compliance is a conformity with external imposed standards to avoid penalties and is driven by external, away from, matching metaprograms. It assumes separate organizations and individuals, all acting independently guided by material self-interest. There is little sense of connection or community. Congruence is self-governing through chosen standards, to enable ethical, value-driven conduct. It has internal, towards metaprograms. It assumes enlightened self-interest on behalf of the organization and its people.

Technology has brought us closer together. We have more influence over wider areas and more idea of systems and how our actions can come back to haunt our children. The value of a business is tied to how the public perceives its stance on topics like pollution and health. The ethical position of companies is also a factor in recruitment. Is the company an attractive prospect?

Managers have to make decisions about right actions from an ethical as well as a technical point of view. Enlightened self-interest means that they have to second position public reaction. It means taking different perspectives. How would I feel about this if I were: the customer . . . the shareholder . . . the supplier . . . a member of the public reading a report of our action in a newspaper? In the UK there is a growing number of companies joining the 'one per cent club'. They are pledged to devote at least one per cent of their profits to charitable causes.

You can do something to create a learning organization and an enterprise culture where people are valued and encouraged to learn and develop their potential, and where they are encouraged to use their ideas and to take action, and are empowered to do so. Then they will be capable of extraordinary work and the organization will achieve extraordinary performance. Start with yourself; you can be part of creating a department and an organization where people want to work, and where you can feel congruent and at home.

FURTHER READING

Ashridge Management College, *Ethics at the Heart of Business*, 1990.
O'Connor, Joseph, and McDermott, Ian, *Principles of NLP*, Thorsons 1996.
Paine, Lynn, 'Managing for organisational integrity', *Harvard Business Review*, March 1994.

NOTE

1   Mintzberg, Henry, *Mintzberg on Management*, Macmillan 1989.

GLOSSARY OF NLP TERMS

Accessing cues   Ways of using our physiology, such as adopting a posture, a way of breathing, or a movement of the eyes, that make it easy to access a particular way of thinking. We are usually unaware of our accessing cues.

Anchor   Any stimulus that is associated with a particular response. May happen naturally, for example, the national anthem, or a red traffic light. May also be set up intentionally, for example, a photograph or piece of music.

Anchoring   Making an association between a stimulus and a response.

'As if' frame   A way to explore future possibilities with questions like: 'What would happen if . . .' or 'Suppose this happened . . .'.

Associated   Being inside an experience, seeing it through our own eyes and experiencing it fully.

Auditory   Relating to the sense of hearing.

Backtracking   Restating a person's key points using mainly their own words. A skill for summarizing, maintaining rapport and gaining commitment.

Behaviour   In NLP used to describe the actions we do, including thinking. Also one of the logical levels.

Beliefs   The generalizations that we make about ourselves, others, and the world. They act as self-fulfilling prophecies that influence all our behaviours. One of the logical levels together with values.

Body language   The way we use our body to communicate. Includes the way we dress, our grooming, posture, and gestures.

Calibrating   Recognizing a person's internal state by reading consistent body language. For example, you notice that on several occasions a person tightens the right side of his face when he disagrees with you. When he does it again you understand he disagrees even though he has said nothing.

Capability   A skill, a consistent successful strategy for carrying out a task. One of the logical levels.

Chunking   Changing perceptions by moving up or down levels. Chunking up – going up and looking at a level that includes what we are studying, for example, the strategic plan that initiated a specific project. Chunking down – going down a level to look at a more specific example or part of what we are studying, for example, the smaller tasks that need to be delegated for a larger project to succeed.

Conditional close   '*If* such and such were to happen, *then* would you . . . ?' Takes the 'As if' frame a little further. Used to test commitment and to explore solutions rather than problems.

Congruence   All parts of our communication are consistently giving the same message – behaviours, words, tonality and body language: 'Walking our talk'. Also means our values and outcomes are aligned.

Criteria   That which is important in a particular context.

Criterial equivalents   The events or behaviours that have to happen for criteria to be met, the rules for their fulfilment.

Crossover matching   Matching a person's body language with a different type of movement, for example, moving your hand in time with their rhythm of speech.

Digital language   Language without sensory predicates, much used in academic, legal and business documents.

Dissociation   Removing yourself from a situation – imagining yourself in an experience rather than being in it. Also thinking about events rather than experiencing them.

Eliciting   The skill of drawing useful information out of others, by getting them to demonstrate behaviourally or tell you what you are seeking. Eliciting may be done verbally or non-verbally.

Emotional state   Also called simply state or internal state. A complex of all our thoughts and feelings, and we are usually aware of it as a dominant emotion.

Environment   Places, people and objects outside ourselves. One of the logical levels.

Eye accessing cues   Movements that correspond with how we think, or what representation system we are using: visual, auditory, or kinesthetic. Sometimes called lateral eye movements.

First position   Experiencing the world from our own point of view and being in touch with our own reality. One of the three main perceptual positions, the others being second position and third position.

Future pacing   Mental rehearsal, imagining doing something in the future to be better able to do it when the need arises.

Identity   Self-image or self-concept. Who people understand themselves to be. One of the logical levels.

In time   Being associated in the 'now' on our timeline.

Incongruence   State of internal dissonance or conflict. Can occur within a person or an organization.

Influence   Affecting others by what we say, our presence and body language. We cannot not influence. Influence is universal and can be premeditated or spontaneous. The purpose of any meeting.

Internal dialogue   Talking to oneself without audibly voicing the words.

Internal representations   All our thoughts and feelings. The mental pictures, sounds, and feelings we remember and create.

Kinesthetic   Relating to the sense of feeling, including touch, emotions and balance.

Leadership   On an individual level, the ability to inspire and motivate others through their own values, to create a community to which they wish to belong. On an organizational level, the ability to translate a vision into action through self and others.

Leading   Having enough rapport through pacing, to change our own behaviour and persuading another person to follow.

Logical levels   Five useful perspectives on an individual or organization: environment, behaviour, capability, belief and identity.

Manipulating   Attempting to produce an outcome that the other person perceives to be at their expense, either during or after the interaction.

Matching   Adopting some aspect of another person's communication style in order to build rapport, for example, their posture. Not the same as mimicry, which is conscious, exact copying of another person's behaviour.

Meta model   A set of language patterns and questions first set out in *The Structure of Magic* by Richard Bandler and John Grinder in 1975. The questions link language with experience. A set of key questions to probe meaning.

Metaphor   A story or figure of speech implying a comparison.

Metaprograms   Habitual, systematic and typically unconscious filters through which we mediate our experience – for example, dealing easily with details rather than generalities, that is, finding it easier to chunk down rather than chunk up.

Mismatching   Adopting different patterns of behaviour from others in order to redirect a meeting or conversation.

Model of the world   How others see, hear and feel their world; a combination of their beliefs, values, emotional states and representational systems. That which allows us to make meaning of our experiences.

Modelling   In NLP, the process of discovering the thoughts and actions that enable others to function as they do. The basis of both NLP and accelerated learning.

Negotiation   The skill of trading off differences to reach an agreement that benefits both parties.

Neuro-Linguistic Programming (NLP)   The study of excellence and a model of the structure of subjective experience.

Nominalization   A verb that has been turned into an abstract noun, for example, management, motivation and education.

Outcome   The result we want and have planned for. Also called goal or objective. In NLP an outcome needs to be stated in the positive, specifies the person's own part in achieving it, is specific enough to have sensory-based evidence, and has been checked for unforeseen consequences.

Pacing Acknowledging another person's reality and building rapport before starting to lead somewhere different. We can pace behaviour, values, beliefs and identity.

Perceptual position The viewpoint we adopt at any moment. In NLP there are three main perceptual positions: your own (first position); someone else's (second position), and an objective observer's (third position).

Positive intention Purpose of a behaviour, that achieves something important for the person who does it.

Predicates Sensory based words that indicate the use of a particular representational system.

Preferred representational system The most accomplished, habitual way of thinking that a person uses.

Rapport The process of building and maintaining a relationship of mutual trust and understanding, by matching words, body language, voice tone, and by pacing values and beliefs. The basis of influence.

Reframing Changing the way of understanding a statement or behaviour to give it another meaning.

Representational systems Internal senses, the ways we think. In NLP there are five main representational systems: visual (sight), auditory (hearing), kinesthetic (feeling), olfactory (smell) and gustatory (taste).

Second position Seeing the world from another person's point of view, and understanding their reality. One of three main perceptual positions.

State See *Emotional state*.

Strategy Sequence of thoughts or behaviour to achieve an outcome.

Systemic thinking Thinking in terms of mutual influence, relationships, and cause and effect separated by time and distance. Seeing the interrelationship between experience or events that seem unconnected. Dealing with complexes of events rather than individual actions in a linear fashion.

Third position   Perceiving the world from the viewpoint of a detached observer. One of the three main perceptual positions.

Through time   Being outside the 'now' on our timeline. A dissociated representation of time, usually where time is a line running from the past on our left, to the future on our right.

Timeline   The way we subjectively represent time as a line running from past to future. A person may be in time when they are in the 'now' and the line passes through their body, or through time where the 'now' is experienced as outside their body.

Values   Those states or experiences that are important to us. One of the logical levels.

Visual   Relating to the sense of sight.

TRAINING AND RESOURCES

A growing number of organizations want to use NLP in their training and staff development. NLP is a significant investment that can give substantial benefits in increased skills and well being, and which requires excellent training from the start. NLP is experiential. We recommend high quality training, where you leave the course being able to practise NLP and not just talk about it.

International Teaching Seminars has pioneered hands-on, skill-based NLP training with practical applications. Software and tapes are also available. For details of the following trainings, software and tapes contact:

> International Teaching Seminars (ITS)
> 73 Brooke Road, London N16 1RD, England
> Tel: 0181 442 4133
> Fax: 0181 442 4155

ITS TRAINING

Open evenings that focus on practical applications of NLP

Fundamentals of NLP

A three-day introduction to NLP and how to use it immediately.

NLP Practitioner Training

A comprehensive programme with a focus on the practical applications of NLP, leading to a fully recognized practitioner certification. No previous training required.

NLP Master Practitioner Training

A complete and fully recognized certification programme with a team of international NLP trainers.

Leadership and Training Programme

How to use NLP to become an effective leader, to present yourself and your ideas powerfully, and to manage relationships.

NLP AUDIOTAPES

The Leadership Programme

Six tapes using advanced NLP techniques for increasing leadership abilities, managing people and presenting yourself powerfully.

Additional sets of tapes are available on related NLP topics. Contact International Teaching Seminars for full details.

MODELLING PROJECTS

Identifying and modelling top performers in the field of business to discover what makes them excel, and designing training to pass on these patterns to others.

ITS CONSULTANCY

The professional application of NLP to the practical needs of large- and small-scale organizations.

Modelling projects and consultancy typically involve:

O   an initial meeting to define your desired outcome, the evidence required for success and the resources needed

O   a needs analysis based on discussions and observations with managers

O   a custom-designed programme developed together – may be modelling key skills, a training programme, a series of workshops or one-on-one coaching sessions

O   review and evaluation.

NLP SOFTWARE

NLP Personal Development Software: Goal Wizard

The first in a suite of Windows-based programs that do not require previous NLP training. Enables you to keep track of individual, team and organizational outcomes, to store them by category, to examine the relationships between them and to clarify them so they are realistic, motivating and achievable. Suitable for personal or business outcomes.

All software works on any IBM compatible PC with Windows 3.1.
For further details phone ITS Software, 0181–442 4133.

PSYCHOLOGICAL SOFTWARE DEVELOPMENT

Many organizations are using software to train communication, negotiation and coaching skills. Joseph O'Connor and Ian McDermott are experienced in designing software to train NLP and communication skills in a way that uses the medium to its fullest capability, with custom-designed applications for specific business problems and organizational development.

CREDITS

We have done our best to track down and credit the sources of the material in this book. Please let us know by mail if we have inadvertently omitted an important source, or if you feel someone is not properly acknowledged. We will do our best to correct future printings.

FEEDBACK

If you have found this book valuable or you have responses or suggestions, we would like to hear from you. We would also be very interested in examples of how using NLP has affected working practice. Please write to us at International Teaching Seminars.

INDEX

Words with asterisk (*) are in the glossary.

197

Brain Sell

Tony Buzan and Richard Israel

All selling is a brain-to-brain process, in which the salesperson's brain communicates with the customer's. Recent new discoveries in the fields of psychology, communication, general science, sports and Olympic training techniques, neurophysiology, brain research, sales research and selling techniques have resulted in *Brain Sell*. In this remarkable book the world's leading expert on harnessing the power of the brain joins forces with a pioneer of modern sales training to show how you can become a high sales producer.

Brain Sell, based on the latest scientific research and the experiences of some of the world's most successful salespeople, explains how to:

• identify which mental skills are currently being used in selling
• apply whole brain selling to any sales situation
• use a multi-sensory format in selling
• develop your sales memory and remember customers' names and faces
• Mind Map and be prepared for the 'sales information age'
• master the mind-body link
• keep focused and retain customer information
• mentally rehearse the sale
• make memorable sales presentations
• develop and use a personal sales commercial.

All of this, together with over 80 skill-building exercises, guarantee a multitude of new ideas in *Brain Sell* for everyone who sells - whatever the type of product or service, and whether you're a beginner or a veteran. Try it!

1995   284 pages   Hardback   0 566 07658 6   Paperback   0 566 07667 5

Gower

Building a Better Team
A Handbook for Managers and Facilitators

Peter D Moxon

Team leadership and team development are central to the modern manager's ability to "achieve results through other people". Successful team building requires knowledge and skill, and the aim of this handbook is to provide both. Using a unique blend of concepts, practical guidance and exercises, the author explains both the why and the how of team development.

Drawing on his extensive experience as manager and consultant, Peter Moxon describes how groups develop, how trust and openness can be encouraged, and the likely problems overcome. As well as detailed advice on the planning and running of teambuilding programmes the book contains a series of activities, each one including all necessary instructions and support material.

Irrespective of the size or type of organization involved, *Building a Better Team* offers a practical, comprehensive guide to managers, facilitators and team leaders seeking improved performance.

| 1993 | 208 pages | 0 566 07424 9 |

Gower

Empowering People at Work

Nancy Foy

This is a book written, says the author, "for the benefit of practical managers coping with real people in real organizations". Part I shows how the elements of empowerment work together: performance focus, teams, leadership and face-to-face communication. Part II explains how to manage the process of empowerment, even in the context of "downsizing" and "delayering". It includes chapters on networking, listening, running effective team meetings, giving feedback, training and using employee surveys. Part III contains case studies of IBM and British Telecom and examines the way they have developed employee communication to help achieve corporate objectives.

The final section comprises a review of communication channels that can be used to enhance the empowerment process, an extensive set of survey questions to be selected on a "pick and mix" basis and an annotated list of useful books.

Empowerment is probably the most important concept in the world of management today, and Nancy Foy's book will go a long way towards helping managers to "make it happen".

| 1994 | 288 pages | 0 566 07436 2 |

Gower

50 Essential Management Techniques

Michael Ward

Are you familiar with the concept of product life cycle? Of course you are! Does the prospect of a SWOT analysis bring you out in a cold sweat? Probably not. But what about the Johari Window? Or Zipf's Law?

Michael Ward's book brings together a formidable array of tools designed to improve managerial performance. For each entry he introduces the technique in question, explains how it works, then goes on to show, with the aid of an entertaining case study, how it can be used to solve an actual problem. The 50 techniques, including some never before published, are grouped into eleven subject areas, ranging from strategy to learning.

For managers in every type of organization and at any level, as well as for students and consultants, *50 Essential Management Techniques* is likely to become an indispensable source.

1995	240 pages	0 566 07532 6

Gower

How to Make Work FUN!
An Alphabet of Possibilities ...

David Firth

With the majority of our lives spent either at work or asleep it seems crazy to consign 'fun' only to life outside of the office. Why do we leave our personalities behind when we set off for work in the morning? Why do we envy people who tell us that their work is fun, yet somehow feel laughter is out of place in the office? And how can we deliver excellent service, or be better than our competitors, if we'd rather not be working at all?

David Firth's totally irreverent book is packed with ideas for banishing boredom and bringing fun to the office. And building stronger teams and increasing productivity in the process ... Find out why you should persuade your company to train your team how to juggle, the benefits of practising saying phrases such as: "Does anyone think that I am bullshitting?", or "Does anybody here know a good joke?", seven new venues for efficient meetings, and what 'KIT' stands for, and why it's a good idea!

This book is a must for anyone who'd like to foster a team spirited positive working environment, get work into perspective (reduce stress levels), or simply enjoy work more. It should be studiously avoided by anyone who feels threatened by the very idea of deriving fun from work.

1995	216 pages	0 566 07712 4

Gower

It's Not Luck

Eliyahu M Goldratt

A Gower Novel

Alex Rogo has had a great year, he was promoted to executive
vice-president of UniCo with the responsibility for three recently
acquired companies. His team of former and new associates is
in place and the future looks secure and exciting. But then
there is a shift of policy at the board level. Cash is needed and
Alex's companies are to be put on the block. Alex faces a cruel
dilemma. If he successfully completes the turnaround of his
companies, they can be sold for the maximum return, but if he
fails, the companies will be closed down. Either way, Alex and
his team will be out of a job. It looks like a lose-lose situation.
And as if he doesn't have enough to deal with, his two children
have become teenagers!

As Alex grapples with problems at work and at home, we begin
to understand the full scope of Eli Goldratt's powerful
techniques, first presented in *The Goal*, the million copy best-
seller that has already transformed management thinking
throughout the Western world. *It's Not Luck* reveals more of
the Thinking Processes, and moves beyond *The Goal* by showing
how to apply them on a comprehensive scale.

This book will challenge you to change the way you think and
prove to you that it's not luck that makes startling
improvements achievable in your life.

1994   288 pages   Hardback   0 566 07637 3   Paperback   0 566 07627 6

Gower

Monkey Business
Why the Way You Manage is a Million Years Out of Date

Gary Johnson

The world of management is a chaotic one. It's hard to know where fashion and fads end and fundamental truths begin. But now there is a way. Today, most people accept evolution as a historical fact. We feel our ape-like ancestors have been left far behind, particularly in our business dealings. In fact, nothing could be further from the truth. Once we get down to doing business, we are all confronted by the same sort of animal - a self-centred business man or woman driven by deep primeval urges. The author points out how often, as business people, we behave exactly as evolutionary theory says we should.

Recent major advances in evolutionary science now make it possible to answer many of the questions that perplex managers the world over. Why are we so often stressed at work and why does this hamper our creativity? What motivates people to learn and co-operate? What drives them to deceive and to become aggressive? What makes some people leaders and other willing followers? What really happens when people communicate face to face?

In this stimulating book Gary Johnson examines these and many other aspects of behaviour, supporting his argument with examples drawn both from research and from business. His approach is certain to appeal to the growing number of managers sceptical of the latest theory or the modish package. They will learn • how to reduce unproductive stress • how to avoid over-reliance on intuition • how to harness people's powers of concentration • how to motivate co-workers • how to manage non-verbal communication.

At once entertaining and illuminating, *Monkey Business* is your guide to the fundamental truths about management as you look back not a few decades, not even a few centuries, but many millennia. It will transform your view of the world of work.

1996   200 pages   0 566 07620 9

Gower

The Motivation Manual

Gisela Hagemann

Improved productivity, flexible work practices, low rates of absenteeism, commitment to quality, ever-higher standards of customer service - these are the benefits of a well-motivated workforce. In this prize-winning book the author takes modern motivational theory and shows how any manager can apply it to create shared vision, develop mutual trust and involve employees in the decision-making process.

The text is enlivened throughout by examples with which managers will identify and there is a unique final section containing twenty seven exercises designed to strengthen interpersonal skills and improve creativity.

"Encouraging reading for individual managers and for those with training responsibilities." **Management in Education**

1992   210 pages   Hardback   0 566 07295 5   Paperback   0 566 07618 7

Gower

Problem Solving in Groups
Second Edition

Mike Robson

Modern scientific research has demonstrated that groups are likely to solve problems more effectively than individuals. As most of us knew already, two heads (or more) are better than one. In organizations it makes sense to harness the power of the group both to deal with problems already identified and to generate ideas for enhancing effectiveness by reducing costs, increasing productivity and the like.

In this revised and updated edition of his successful book, Mike Robson first introduces the concepts and methods involved. Then, after setting out the advantages of the group approach, he examines in detail each of the eight key problem solving techniques. The final part of the book explains how to present proposed solutions, how to evaluate results and how to ensure that the group process runs smoothly.

With its practical tone, its down-to-earth style and lively visuals, this is a book that will appeal strongly to managers and trainers looking for ways of improving their organization's and their department's performance.

1993   176 pages   Hardback   0 566 07414 1   Paperback   0 566 07415 X

Gower